THE BIG
ENIGMA

THE BIG
ENIGMA

Scripture quotations are from the ESV Bible (The Holy Bible, English Standard Version), copyright © 2001 by Crossway Bibles, a publishing ministry of Good News Publishers. Used by permission. All rights reserved.

ISBN 978-1948109116
LCCN 2019935457
Proofreading: Jussara Korngold
Book design: Helton Mattar Monteiro
Cover design: Mauro de Souza Rodrigues

International data for cataloging in publication (CIP)

D395be Denis, Léon, 1846–1927.
      The big enigma: God and the universe / Léon Denis.
      Translator: Helton Mattar Monteiro. – New York: United States
      Spiritist Council, 2019.
      219 pp.; 21.59 cm.

      Original title: La grand énigme: Dieu et l'univers (last rev. ed., 1921;
      and a recent version for supplemental notes nos. 4, 5, 6 and 7).

      ISBN: 978-1948109116

      1. Metaphysics. 2. Spiritism. 3. New Spiritualism. I. Title. II. Title.

      LCCN: 2019935457   DDC 133.93   UDC 133.7

1st edition, 1st print – March 2019

LÉON DENIS

THE BIG ENIGMA

GOD AND THE UNIVERSE

TRANSLATED BY H. M. MONTEIRO

UNITED STATES SPIRITIST FEDERATION
NEW YORK
2019

CONTENTS

TO THE READER

At hard times in life, in days of sadness and distress, do open this book! With echoes of voices from above, it will give you courage; it will inspire patience, bringing acceptance of the eternal laws!

Where and how did I think of writing it? It was during a winter evening, an evening of walks along the azure coast of Provence in southern France.

The sun was setting on the calm sea. Its golden rays, gliding over the sleeping valleys, lit burning hues on the tops of rocks and promontories, while a thin lunar crescent climbed into the cloudless sky. A great silence was enveloping everything. Only a distant bell, slowly, tolled the Angelus.

Absorbed in my thoughts, I heard muffled sounds, the barely perceptible rumors of the partying winter towns, and the voices that sang in my soul.

I thought of the merriment of fellow human beings who intoxicate themselves with pleasure so as to better forget the purpose of life, its imperious duties and heavy responsibilities. The lullaby sea, the sky which little by little was studded with stars, the penetrating scents of myrtle and pine, the distant harmonies in the stillness of evening, all contributed to spreading in and around me a subtle charm, both intimate and deep.

Then a voice said to me: publish a book that we will inspire you with, a little book that summarizes all that the human soul must know in order to orient itself through its path. Publish a book that shows to all that life is not a plaything that we can use with levity, but rather a struggle for conquering heaven, a high and serious work of edification and perfectionment; a work governed by noble and equitable laws, above which eternal Justice hovers, tempered by Love.

Justice! If there is in this world a need, an imperative necessity for all those who suffer, whose souls are torn apart, that is the need to believe, to know for sure that justice is not an empty word, that somewhere there is compensation for all our pains, a sanction for all duties, a consolation for all evils.

Now, this absolute, sovereign justice, whatever your political opinions and social views may be, is admittedly not in our world. Human institutions do not include or offer it.

And even if we manage to correct and improve such institutions, and later, to mitigate many evils, to reduce the sum of human inequalities and miseries, there are still causes of affliction, such as cruel and innate infirmities against which we will always be impotent: the loss of health, of sight, of sanity; the separation of loved ones; and all the immense procession of moral suffering, all the more vivid as humans become more sensitive and civilization more refined.

Despite all social improvements, we will never witness either good or evil find their full reward or penalty here below. If there is an absolute, integral justice, it can only be found in the afterlife! But who will prove to us that this life beyond is not a myth, an illusion, a chimera? Religions and philosophies have passed which displayed on the human soul the rich cloak of their conceptions and their hopes. However, doubt has subsisted deep in our souls. A careful and scholarly critique has sifted through all theories of yesteryear. And from their majestic whole only ruins have remained.

But then, on all points of the globe, psychical phenomena started to occur. They were various, continual, innumerable, and brought proof of the existence of a spiritual world, invisible and governed by rigorous principles as immutable as those of matter; a world which conceals in its depths the secret of our origins and destinies.[1] Thus a new science is born, based on the experiments, investigations, and testimonies of eminent scholars. Through it, a communication has been established with the unseen world that surrounds us, and a powerful revelation has flown to humanity as a pure and regenerative wave.

Perhaps never before in the course of its history has France felt more deeply the desirability of a new moral orientation. As said above, religions have lost much of their prestige, and the poisoned fruits of materialism are now everywhere. Alongside the selfishness and sensuality of some there is also the brutality and greed of others. Violence, murder and suicide are on the rise. Strikes are becoming more and more tragic. It is the class struggle, unleashing appetites and fury. The populace's voice is rising and roaring; the hatred of the little ones toward those who possess and enjoy all riches tends to move from the realm of theories into that of reality. Barbarous practices, destructive of all civilization, have penetrated some working-class members. Factories are sacked, machines broken, industrial equipment sabotaged. Should this state of affairs worsen, it would bring us straight back to civil war and savagery.

---

[1] See also Léon DENIS, *Into the Unseen* (Trans. H. M. Monteiro. New York: USSF, 2017); and *Christianisme et Spiritisme* (New ed. Paris: Librairie de Sciences Psychiques, 1910).

This is the result of a false national education. For centuries, neither schools nor churches have taught the people what they most need to know: the reason of existence, the law of destiny with a true sense of duties and accountabilities attached to it. Hence this turmoil of minds and consciences, this overall confusion, this demoralization and anarchy which abound both high and low in all walks of life. We are under the threat of social collapse. Will it be necessary to descend to the bottom of the abyss of public miseries, in order to realize the error we made and understand that we must seek above all a ray of light that can illuminate the great human march on the winding road, through swamps and crumbled rocks?

November 1910

PART ONE

GOD AND THE UNIVERSE

I

THE BIG ENIGMA

I s there a real goal, a law, in the universe? Or is it merely an abyss in which thought is lost for lack of a supporting reference; or spinning on itself like a dead leaf under the gusts of wind?

Is there a force, a hope, a certainty that can raise us above ourselves to a higher goal, a principle, a level of being in which good, truth and wisdom can be identified; or else, only doubt, uncertainty, and darkness exist in and around us?

Humans, thinkers among us, examine the vast expanse, questioning the depths of the sky. There they seek the solution of two great problems: the problem of the world and the problem of life. They ponder about this majestic universe, in which we feel as if drowned. They follow with their eyes the trajectory of the giants of space, the suns of the night, terrifying fires whose light travels through the bleak immensities. We interrogate the stars, the innumerable orbs; yet they move on, silently pursuing their path toward a goal we cannot fathom. A crushing silence hovers over the abyss that envelops the human race, making this universe take on an ever more solemn character.[2]

Yet, at first sight, two things present themselves to us in the universe: matter and movement, substance and force. The worlds are formed of matter, and this matter, inert by itself, moves. What makes it move? What is this force that drives it? This is our first problem. Then humans,

---

2 This silence is relative and results only from the imperfection of our senses.

from the infinite, carry their attention back to themselves. Such universal matter and force, we find within ourselves and with them a third element, with the help of which we have come to know, see, and measure the other ones: our intelligence.

All the same, human intelligence is not in itself its own cause. If the human being were its own cause, it could keep and preserve the power of life that is in itself; whereas this power is in fact subject to all sorts of variations and failures, escaping human will.

$$\approx$$

If intelligence exists in human beings, then it must also exist in this universe of which it is an integral part. What exists in the component must also be in the whole. Matter is only our clothing, the sensitive and changing form with which we are clad in life: a corpse cannot think or move. Force is a simple agent called on to keep the vital functions. Therefore it is intelligence that governs the worlds and rules the universe

This intelligence is manifested in laws, both wise and profound, for the order and conservation of the cosmos.

All the researches, all the works of contemporary science, concur to demonstrate the action of natural laws, which a supreme law connects and encompasses in order to form the universal harmony. By this law, a sovereign intelligence is revealed as the very reason of all things; a conscious reason, universal unity toward where all relations converge, connect and merge; and where all beings come to draw strength, light and life; the absolute and perfect being, immutable foundation and eternal source of all science, truth and wisdom; of all love.

Nevertheless, some objections are to be expected. It may be said, for instance, that theories on matter, force, and intelligence, as formerly formulated in scientific and philosophical circles, have had their day. New concepts have come to replace them. Current physics shows us that matter dissociates itself from analysis and resolves itself into force centers, while force itself gets absorbed in the universal ether.

Indeed, surely those systems are aging and passing; formulas are wearing out; but the eternal idea resurfaces with the emergence of ever new and richer forms. Materialism and Spiritualism are both transient aspects of knowledge. Neither matter nor spirit is what the old schools of thought they were – and perhaps matter, thought, and life are linked by close bonds that only now we are beginning to glimpse.

Still, some facts remain and other problems arise. Matter and force are absorbed in the ether; but what is the ether? It is, we are told, the raw material, the final substratum of every movement. The ether itself is traversed by innumerable motions: luminous and calorific radiations, electric and magnetic currents. Now, these motions must be regulated in certain ways.

Force generates movement, but force itself is not a law. Blind and guideless, it could never produce order and harmony in the universe. These are, however, evident. At the top of the scale of forces, mental energy, willpower and intelligence arise, which build forms and sets laws.[3]

---

3 Despite his reluctance, G. LEBON (or LE BON), in his *Evolution of Matter* (Trans. F. Legge. London and New York: Walter Scott Pub. Co. Ltd. & C. Scribner's Sons, 1907), book VI, ch. VI, p. 295, is forced to admit that, "All these operations, so precise, so admirably adapted to one purpose, are directed by forces of which we have no conception, which

In addition, I must say: inertia is only relative, since matter is concrete energy. In reality, all the constitutive particles of a body move. However, the energy stored in these bodies can only become effective if the material component is dissociated. This is not the case of planets, whose elements represent matter at its last degree of concretion. Their movements cannot be explained by an internal force, but rather only by the intervention of an external energy.

"Inertia," says G. Lebon, "is the resistance of unknown cause that bodies oppose to movement or change of motion. It is capable of being measured, and it is this measure which is defined by the term mass. Mass is therefore the measure of the inertia of matter, its coefficient of resistance to movement."[4]

From Pythagoras to Claude Bernard, all thinkers say that matter is devoid of spontaneity. Any attempt to lend to the inert substance a spontaneity capable of organizing and explaining force has failed.

Therefore, one must necessarily return to the concept of a first transcendent motor, in order to explain the system of the cosmos. Celestial mechanics cannot be explained by itself, and the existence of an initial motor is essential. The primitive nebula, mother of the sun and planets, was animated by a whirling motion. But who had imparted this movement to it? The answer without hesitation is God.

act exactly as if they possessed a power of clairvoyance very superior to reason. What they accomplish every moment of our existence is far above what can be realized by the most advanced science."

[4] In *Revue Scientifique*, Paris, October 17, 1903.

Is it only contemporary science that reveals God, the universal Being, to us? Let us interrogate Earth's history. It evokes the memory of multitudes of deceased people, of generations that now lie under the dust of centuries. Let us interrogate the credulous faith of the simple and the reasoned faith of the learned: Everywhere, above contradictory opinions and disputes among different schools of thought; above rivalries of social classes, interests and passions; we will find the drives and aspirations of human thought toward a cause; the great cause which watches over, solemn and silent, under the mysterious veil of things.

At all times and in all walks of life, the human complaint has risen to that Divine Spirit, to that Soul of the world honored with so many names. Under various designations, such as Providence, our heavenly Creator, the Great Architect, the Supreme Being, and so on, has always been the Fulcrum, the Law, the universal Reason by means of which the world gets to know itself, takes possession of itself, and regains consciousness and awareness of its own self.

And thus, in the universe, above this incessant ebb and flow of transient and changing elements, above all variety and infinite diversity of beings and things – which constitute the domain of Nature and life – thought encounters that fixed and unchangeable principle, that conscious unity in which essence and substance are united. It is the primary source of all consciousnesses and forms, for consciousness and form, essence and substance, cannot exist without each other. They unite to constitute this living unity, this absolute and necessary Being, source of all beings, which we call God.

But human language is powerless to express the idea of an infinite Being. As soon as we use names and terminologies, we limit what is limitless. All definitions are insufficient, and to some extent misleading. However, thought, in order to express itself, has to use terms. The least remote from reality seems to be that by which the priests of Ancient Egypt designated God: *I am*; that is to say, I am the Being par excellence, absolute, eternal, from which all beings emanate.

A centuries-old misunderstanding divides philosophical schools on these issues. Materialism sees in the universe only substance and force. It seems to ignore the etherealized[5] states, the infinite transformations of matter. Traditional Spiritualism[6] still sees in God only the spiritual principle. It considers as immaterial all that does not fall under our senses. Yet, both are mistaken. The misunderstanding that separates them will not cease until materialists see in their principle, and traditional Spiritualists see in their God, the source of the three elements: substance, force, and intelligence, whose unity constitutes universal life.

To achieve this, it suffices to understand two things: if one admits that substance is outside God, then God is not infinite; and since consciousness exists in the current world, it must obviously have been present before in what was the Principle, the Origin of this world.

Yet current science, after lingering for half a century in the wilderness of materialism and positivism, and eventually recognizing their fruitlessness, has now completely changed its orientation. With a firm step, it is moving in every

---

5 [Trans. note] "*Quintessenciés*" in the original. The English term *etherealized* is more current than *quintessenced*, which however has some old philosophical implications (please check the unabridged edition of the *Oxford English Dictionary*).

6 [Trans. note] As opposed to *Spiritism* or "New Spiritualism" (in Léon DENIS' parlance).

field – physics, chemistry, biology, psychology – toward a great unity that is glimpsed at the core of everything. Everywhere science is now acknowledging the unity of substance, the unity of forces, the unity of laws. Behind all molten substance there lies strength; and force is nothing but the projection of thought, of the will, into substance. Therefore, eternal creation, as an eternal renewal of beings and things, is nothing more than the constant projection of God's thought into the universe.

Gradually the veil is lifted, and we humans begin to glimpse the magnificent plan of life evolution on the surface of the worlds. We see the correlation of forces and the adaptation of forms and organs in all different environments. We know that life develops, transforms and refines itself as it goes through this immense spiral. We realize that everything is planned and shaped toward a purpose, which is the continuous improvement of the living soul, and the increase of the sum of good and beauty that lies in it.

Even here below, we can follow this majestic law of progress throughout the slow labor of Nature, from the most inferior forms of being, from desmids (microscopic algae) floating in the water, to conscious humans in whom the unity of life asserts itself; and the forms above them, climbing step by step to infinity. And such an ascension can only be understood or explained by the existence of a universal principle, of an unceasing, eternal energy, which pervades all nature. It is this principle which regulates and stimulates the colossal evolution of beings and worlds toward a better future, and the ultimate good.

God, as conceived by us, is neither the God of Oriental pantheism, which is confused with the universe; nor the anthropomorphic God, monarch of Heaven, outside the world, as preached by the Western religions of the world. God is manifested by the universe which is Its representation as perceived by the senses, but does not merge with it. Just as within us the conscious unity – the soul, the self – persists in the midst of perpetual changes of corporeal matter, so, in the midst of the transformations of the universe, and the incessant renewal of its components, the immutable Being remains, which is the soul, the consciousness, the self which animates it, imparting movement and life to it.

And this great Being, absolute and eternal, which knows our needs, hears our appeals, our prayers, and is sensitive to our pains, is like an immense fulcrum where all beings, by communion of thought and feeling, come to draw the forces, the reinforcements, the inspirations necessary to guide them in the paths of their destinies, to support them in their struggles, to comfort them in their miseries, to raise them up after their failures and tumbles.

Do not seek God in temples of stone and marble, O fellow human beings who wish to know It, but in the eternal temple of Nature instead, in the spectacle offered by the worlds traveling the infinite expanse of space, in the splendors of life which flourishes in their surface, in the view of varied horizons: plains, valleys, mountains and seas, such as we have in our earthly dwelling. Everywhere, under the light of day or the starry cloak of nights, on the edge of tumultuous oceans or in the solitude of forests, if you know how to withdraw yourself into an inner retreat, you will hear the voices of Nature and the subtle teachings it whispers in the ears of those who venture to penetrate its recesses and study its mysteries.

The Earth moves silently in space. This mass close to 8,000 miles in diameter slides on the waves of the ether like a bird in space, like a tiny gnat in the light. Nothing betrays its imposing march. No squeaks of wheels, no murmur of waves beating against its flanks. Quietly, it travels, revolving among its fellow orbs in deep space. All the mighty machine of the universe is agitated, all the millions of suns and worlds that compose it, worlds near which ours is only a speckle. All moving and passing by one another, they pursue their revolutions with frightening speeds, without any sound or clash betraying the action of this gigantic device. The universe remains calm. It is the absolute equilibrium. It is the majesty of a mysterious power, of an intelligence that does not impose itself, but rather hides itself in the midst of things, revealing its presence to thought and to our hearts, and attracting the seeker like an infinite abyss.

If the Earth moved noisily; if the mechanism of the universe went up with a bang, we humans, weighed down by fear, would kneel and be forced to believe. Yet no! The formidable work of the universe is accomplished without effort. Globes and suns float in the infinite cosmos, as light as feathers in the breeze. Forward, always ahead, the circle of spheres unfolds, guided by an invisible power!

The will that directs the universe is hidden from all eyes. Things are arranged in such a way that no one is forced to believe in it. If the order and harmony of the cosmos are not enough to convince humans, they remain free to choose. Nothing compels the skeptic to go to God.

It is the same when it comes to moral things. Our existences unfold and the events succeed one another without any apparent connection. But immanent justice hangs high above us and regulates our destinies according to an ineluctable principle, by which everything is linked in a series of causes and effects. Together they constitute a harmony that any spirit freed from prejudice, once enlightened by a ray of wisdom, discovers and admires.

What do we know about the universe? Our eyes can perceive only a limited portion of the empire of things. Only material bodies, similar to us, impress our sight. Subtle and diffuse matter escapes our perception.[7] We only see what the coarsest matter on our plane. All the fluidic worlds, all the circles in which the superior life moves, and radiant life, escape the human sight. We can only discern the opaque and heavy worlds that move in the cosmos. The space between them seems empty to us. Everywhere, deep abysses seem to open. What an error! The universe is full. Between these material dwellings, in the gaps between these planetary worlds, prisons or penal colonies floating in space, and other domains of life unfold, spiritual life, glorious life that our thick senses cannot detect, because if exposed to their radiations, they would crack like glass under the impact of a stone.

Wise Nature has restricted our powers of perception and sensation. Only gradually, it leads us on the path of knowledge. It is slowly, step by step, from lifetime to lifetime, that it leads us to the knowledge of the universe, whether visible or unseen. Beings climb one by one the steps of the gigantic staircase that leads to God. And each of these degrees entails a long series of centuries for us.

If celestial worlds appeared to us suddenly, without veils, in all their glory, we would be dazzled and blinded. However, our external senses have been graded and limited. They grow and become more refined as the self rises on the scale of existences and improvements. It is the same with knowledge, with becoming aware of moral laws. The universe gradually unfolds before our eyes as our ability to understand the laws increases. An unhurried incubation of souls is carried out under the divine light.

---

[7] At our current stage of development, we do not know and cannot know either spirit or matter in their essence.

~~

It is toward you, O Supreme Power! Whatever name you are given, and however imperfectly you are understood, it is to you, eternal source of life, beauty and harmony, that we raise all our aspirations, all our yearnings, our trust, and our love!

Where are You? In what deep, mysterious heavens are You hidden? How many souls thought it would be enough to leave the Earth in order to meet You! But you remain invisible in the spiritual world as here in the earthly world, invisible to those who have not yet attained sufficient purity to reflect your divine rays. Nonetheless, everything reveals and manifests Your presence. All that, in Nature and in humanity, sings and celebrates love, beauty, perfection, all that lives and breathes is a message from God. The great forces that animate the universe proclaim the reality of divine intelligence; beside them, the majesty of God has been manifested in history by the action of great souls, who, like huge tidal waves, bring to earthly shores all the powers generated by deeds of wisdom and love.

And God is also in each and every one of us, in the living temple of conscience. This is the sacred place, the sanctuary where the divine spark hides.

Fellow human beings! Learn to withdraw into yourselves and look. Search the innermost folds of your being, interrogate yourself in silence and retreat, and you will get to know yourself, to know the power hidden inside you. It is this power that rises and shines in the depths of our consciences bringing up holy images of goodness, truth and justice. And it is by honoring these divine projections, by revering them everyday, that our consciousness and conscience, still obscure, will be purified and illuminated. Gradually, light will increase in us. As the dawn succeeds the night, as gradually, imperceptibly, the shadows give way to the brightness of the day, so the soul is illuminated by the radiations of this core that lies in it, and that gives birth in our thought and heart to perpetually renewed, ever inexhaustible forms of truth and beauty. This light is also a penetrating harmony, a voice that sings in the soul of the poet, of the writer, of the prophet, inspiring them and dictating to them the great and strong texts through which they work for the elevation of humanity. They alone feel these things which, once they have mastered matter, make worthy of sublime communion all those whose inner sense has opened itself to deep impressions and who know, after ages-old efforts, the powerful breath which fuels the fires of genius; the breath that passes over pensive brows and makes our human envelopes shudder.

II

SUBSTANTIAL UNITY OF THE UNIVERSE

The universe is one, though tripartite in appearance. Spirit, force, and matter seem to be only modes, the three states of a substance which is immutable in its principle, albeit infinitely variable in its manifestations.

The universe lives and breathes animated by two powerful currents, namely, absorption and diffusion. Through this expansion, through this immense breath, God, the Being of beings, the Soul of the universe, effects creation. By Its love, God draws everything to itself. The vibrations of Its thought and will, primary sources of all cosmic forces, move the universe and engender life.

Matter, as mentioned above, is only a mode, a transient form of the universal substance. It escapes analysis and disappears under the lens of microscopes, to resolve itself into subtle radiations. It does not have an existence per se; the philosophies that take it as a basis have rested on mere appearance, on a sort of illusion.[8]

The unity of the universe as a whole, long denied or misunderstood, is beginning to be grasped by science. Twenty years ago, during his studies on the materialization of spirits, British scientist William Crookes discovered the fourth state of matter, the radiant state; and this discovery, by its consequences, was to upset all the old classical theories. These made a distinction between matter and force. Now

---

[8] "Matter is but a mode of motion," said W. CROOKES (*Proceedings of the Royal Society*, vol. XXX, p. 472, London, 1880).

we know that both are merged. Under the action of heat, the coarsest matter is transformed into fluids; these fluids in turn are reduced to a more subtle element that escapes our senses. Any matter can be reduced into force, and any force can be condensed into matter, thus going through an incessant cycle.[9]

The experiments of Sir W. Crookes have been continued and confirmed by a group of researchers. The most famous of them, Roentgen, called X-rays the radiation emanating from vacuum glass tubes. Such rays have the property of crossing through most opaque bodies, thus allowing us to perceive and photograph the invisible.

Shortly thereafter, French physicist Henri Becquerel demonstrated the properties of certain metals of emitting obscure radiations which are able to penetrate the densest matter, such as the so-called Rœntgen rays, even impressing photographic plates through metal plates.

Radium, discovered by Madame Curie, produces heat and light in a continuous manner, without suffering any significant loss of substance. The bodies subjected to its action become themselves radiant.[10] Although the quantity of energy radiated by this metal is considerable, the loss of material substance which corresponds to it is almost nil. W. Crookes calculated that it would take a hundred years for one gram of radium to disintegrate.[11]

There is still much more. The ingenious discoveries of French polymath G. Le Bon have proved that radiations are a property common to all bodies. Matter can dissociate

---

[9] W. CROOKES later added that all matter has to pass through the ethereal state from which it comes (address given at the Fifth Congress of Applied Chemistry, Berlin, 1903). [Trans. note: The concept of *ether* and *ethereal state* comes straight from pre-atomic physics, which served as basis for most of L. DENIS's theoretical analysis on matter and force.]

[10] [Trans. note] Nowadays we would say *radioactive*. Note that the lethal dangers of radium and radioactivity were still largely unknown.

[11] See G. LE BON, *Revue Scientifique*, October 24, 1903, p. 518.

indefinitely; it is just solidified energy. Thus the theory of the indivisible atom, which for two thousand years had served as a basis for physics and chemistry, collapses and, with it, the classical distinctions between the ponderable and the imponderable.[12] Thus ends the sovereignty of matter once thought to be absolute and eternal.

Thus it must be acknowledged that the universe is not as it appears to be to our feeble senses. The physical world is only a small part of it. Beyond the range of our perception, there are innumerable subtle forces and forms that science has ignored so far. The realm of the invisible is much vaster and richer than that of the visible world.

In its analysis of the elements that make up the universe, science has wandered for centuries, and now must destroy what it has painfully constructed. The scientific dogma of the irreducible and indestructible unity of the atom has collapsed, bringing with it all the materialistic theories. The existence of fluids, affirmed by Spiritists since the mid-1800s – and which earned them much derision from official scholars – has now been established through rigorous experimentation.

Living beings, too, emit radiations of different natures. Human emanations, varying in form and intensity under the action of the will, impress photographic plates with their mysterious light. These impulses, whether nervous or psychical, long known to magnetizers and Spiritists, but denied by science, are now being irrefutably observed by physiologists as a reality. These caused the principle of telepathy to be discovered. Volitions of thought and projections of the will are transmitted through space, like

---

12 For centuries, the theory of atoms has been affirmed and defended without any knowledge. BERTHELOT describes it as an "ingenious and subtle novel." (BERTHELOT, *La Synthèse Chimique*, 1876, p. 164). By this we see, says LE BON, that certain scientific dogmas have no more substance than the deities of antiquity. [Trans. note: also *cf.* note 9 above.]

the vibrations of sound and the waves of light, going to impress organisms in tune with that of the manifesting agent. Souls in affinity of thought and feeling can exchange their emanations at all distances, in the same way that the stars exchange their flickering rays through deep space. Here again we discover the secret of ardent sympathies or invincible repulsions that certain individuals experience for one another from the first time they meet.

Most psychological problems: suggestion, communication at a distance, hidden actions and reactions, vision through obstacles, can be explained. We are still only at the dawn of true knowledge. But the research field is largely open, and science will go from conquest to conquest on a path full of surprises. The invisible world is revealed as the very basis of the universe, and as the eternal source of the physical and vital energies that animate the cosmos.

Thus falls the main argument of those who denied the possibility of the existence of spirits. They could not conceive of an invisible life, for want of a *substratum* (a foundation, a basis) of a substance beyond our common senses. Now we find at the same time, in the realm of imponderables, the constitutive elements of the life of these spirit beings and the forces which are necessary for them to manifest their existence.

Spiritist phenomena of all kinds can be explained by the fact that a considerable and constant expenditure of energy can occur without any apparent loss of matter. Apports,[13] spontaneous disintegration and reconstitution of objects in closed rooms; cases of levitation, passage of spirits through solid bodies, apparitions and materializations, which formerly caused so much astonishment and aroused so many taunts, have now become far easier to admit and

---

[13] (Trans. note) Also referred to as *apportation* or *apporting*, nowadays popularly known as *teleportation* of physical objects.

understand, as people become aware of the forces and elements that come into play in these phenomena. Such dissociations of matter, noted by Dr. Gustave Lebon, and which humans are still powerless to produce, have for a long time been employed by spirits that know their rules and laws.

Does not the application of X-rays in photography also explain the phenomenon of second vision of mediums and also spirit photography? Indeed, if plates can be influenced by dark rays, by radiations of imponderable matter which penetrate opaque bodies, with all the more reason would etherealized fluids, which compose the envelope of every spirit, be able to impress, under certain conditions, the retina of seers, which is a far more delicate and complex apparatus than the glass plate used by photographers.

It is thus that Spiritism gets stronger by the day, with the addition of arguments drawn from scientific discoveries, and which will eventually shake even the most hardened skeptics.

—————

The great quarrel that has divided philosophical schools for centuries is thus reduced to a matter of terminology. In the experiments conducted by Sir William Crookes, matter melts, the atom vanishes; in their place, energy appears. Substance is a Proteus (a shapeshifter) that has a thousand unexpected forms. The gases, which were considered permanent, can liquefy; the air is decomposed into far more numerous elements than the science of yesterday taught it could; and radioactivity, that is, the ability of bodies to disintegrate by emitting cathodic rays, has now proved to be a universal fact. A revolution is taking place in the fields of physics and chemistry. Everywhere around us, we see the opening of sources of energy, immense reservoirs of forces,

far superior in power to all that we knew hitherto.[14] Science
is gradually moving toward the great unitary synthesis,
which is a fundamental law of Nature. His most recent
discoveries have an incalculable significance, in that they
demonstrate experimentally the great constitutive principle
of the universe: the unity of forces, the unity of laws. A
prodigious sequence of forces and beings becomes more
accurate and complete. We see that there is an absolute
continuity, not only among all the states of matter, but also
between them and the different states of force.[15]

Energy seems to be the substance, unique and universal.
In its compact state, it takes on the appearances we call
matter: solid, liquid, and gaseous. In a more subtle state,
it constitutes the phenomena of light, heat, electricity,
magnetism, and chemical affinity. In studying the action of
the will upon emanations and radiations, we could perhaps
catch a glimpse of the point, the summit where the force
becomes intelligent, where the law is manifested, where
thought is changed into life.

Because everything is interconnected and linked in the
universe. Everything is regulated by the laws of number,
measure, and harmony. The highest manifestations of energy
are reserved to intelligence. Force becomes attraction, which
becomes love. Everything is summed up in a unique and
primordial power, an eternal and universal motor, which
have been called various names and which is none other but
thought, the divine will. Its vibrations animate the infinite.

---

14 See supplemental note no. 2 at the end of this book.

15 "The products of the dissociation of atoms," says G. Lebon,
"constitute an intermediary substance with its properties between
ponderable bodies and imponderable ether, that is to say, between
two worlds so far apart up to now." (*Revue Scientifique*, October 17,
1903). "The preceding observations," says the eminent chemist, "seem
to prove that the various simple bodies derive from a single matter. This
primitive matter would be produced by a condensation of the ether."
(*Revue Scientifique*, October 24, 1903). [Excerpts trans. by H.M.M.].

All beings, all worlds, are bathed in the ocean of radiation that emanate from this inexhaustible core.

Aware of their ignorance and weakness, humans remain confused before this formidable unity which embraces all things and carries with it the life of all civilizations. However, at the same time, the study of the universe opens deep sources of enjoyment and emotion to human beings. Despite our intellectual infirmity, whatever little we can perceive of universal laws delights us, for, in the ordering power of laws and worlds, we perceive God, and thereby obtain the certainty that good, beauty, and perfect harmony reign supreme over everything.

III

SOLIDARITY: UNIVERSAL COMMUNION

God is the spirit of wisdom, love and life, the infinite power that governs the world. We humans are finite, but we have the intuition of the infinite. The spiritual principle that we carry in us encourages us to look into problems that go beyond the limits of our current comprehension. Our spirit, imprisoned in the flesh, sometimes emerges from it and rises toward the higher domains of thought, from which these lofty aspirations come, too often followed by relapses into matter. Hence so much research, trial and error, so much so that it would be impossible for us to discern truth in the maze of systems and superstitions that the work of the ages has built up, should the invisible powers fail to come in order to throw some light in this chaos.

Each soul is a ray of the great universal soul, a spark emanating from the eternal core. Yet we ignore ourselves, and this ignorance is the cause of our feebleness and all our ills.

We are united to God in the close connection that binds cause and effect; and we are as necessary to Its existence as It is necessary to ours. God, the universal Spirit, manifests itself in Nature, and humans are, on Earth, the highest expression of Nature. We are the work and expression of God, the source of all good. But this good, we possess it only in the embryonic state. Our task is to develop it. Our successive lives, our ascension in the infinite spiral of existences, have no other goal.

In the depths of the souls, everything lies written in mysterious characters: the past, from which we emerge and which we must learn to probe; the future toward which we are moving, a future we will build ourselves as a wondrous monument, made of lofty thoughts, noble deeds, devotion and self-sacrifice.

The work that each of us must accomplish can be summed up in three words: to know, to believe, and to wish; that is to say: to know that we have incalculable resources within ourselves; to believe in the efficacy of our actions upon the two realms of matter and spirit; to wish good by directing our thoughts toward beauty and greatness, conforming our actions to the eternal laws of work, justice and love.

Originated from God, all souls are siblings; all children of the human race are bound by close ties of loving fellowship and solidarity. Also, the progress of each one of us is felt by all of us, just as the degradation of one of us affects all the rest.

Human brotherhood and sisterhood derives from God's parenthood; all the rapports that unite us are related to this fact. God, parent of all souls, must be regarded as the conscious Being par excellence and not as an abstraction. Nevertheless, anyone who has a righteous conscience and is enlightened by a ray from above, already acknowledges God and serves It within the humanity that is Its offspring and Its work.

When human beings become aware of their true nature and their unity with God, when this notion has penetrated their reason and their heart, they rise to the supreme truth, dominating from above all earthly vicissitudes. They find the strength that can "move mountains," and make them victorious in their struggle against passions, while disregarding disappointments and death. Such humans are able to accomplish what is popularly termed prodigies. Through their willpower and faith, they subjugate and govern reality; they break the fatalities of matter; they are regarded almost as gods by other humans. Several individuals, in their passage here below, have reached these heights of thought. Only Christ has reached the pinnacle, to the point of daring to say in the face of all people: "I and the Father are one." (John 10:30 ESV) "I am in the Father and the Father is in me ..." (John 14:10)

These words, however, did not apply to him alone; they are true regarding all humanity. Christ knew that every human being must come to understand their inner nature, and it is in this sense that he said to his disciples, "You are gods." (John 10:34) He could have added: Gods in the making!

The ignorance of our own nature and the divine forces that lie asleep in us, the insufficient idea that we have of our role and of the laws of destiny, make us prey to inferior influences, which we call evil. In reality, evil is just a lack of development. The state of ignorance is not an evil by itself; it is only one of the forms – a necessary condition – of the law of evolution. Our intelligence is not mature; our infant reason stumbles across obstacles on the road; hence the errors, the failures, the trials, the pain. Yet all these things can be good if we consider them as part of our education and elevation. The soul must overcome them in order to arrive at the conception of higher truths, taking possession of its share of glory and light that will make it an elect of heaven, a perfect expression of infinite power and love. Each being has the rudiments of an intelligence that will reach the level of a genius; and it has the immensity of the time at its disposal, to develop it. Every earthly lifetime is a school, the elementary school of eternity.

In the slow ascension that brings all beings to God, what we seek above all is bliss, happiness. However, in our state of ignorance, we cannot achieve them, for we almost always look for them where they are not, in a region of delusions, mirages and chimeras, by means of processes whose falsity only reveals itself after many disappointments and pains. Such sufferings ultimately enlighten us – our pains are austere lessons – by teaching us that true happiness does not lie in the transient and changing material world, but in moral perfection. Our constant errors and mistakes, with the fatal consequences they entail, end up giving us experience, and this leads us to wisdom, that is, innate knowledge, intuition of the truth. Once gaining this solid foothold, humans can feel the bond which unites them with God, and advance more assuredly, step by step, toward the great light that never goes out.

～

All beings are connected to each other and influence each other. The entire universe is subject to the law of solidarity.

The worlds lost in the depths of the ether, the stars which, at millions of leagues apart, intersect their silvery rays, know each other, call each other, and answer one another. A force we call attraction unites them through the abysses of space.

Likewise, on the ladder of life, all souls are united by multiple relationships. The solidarity that binds them is based on the identity of their nature, on the equality of their sufferings over time, on the similarity of their destinies and their ends.

Like the stars in heaven, all these souls attract one another. Matter exerts its mysterious powers over the spirit. Like Prometheus on his rock, it connects him to the dark worlds. The human soul feels all the attractions of inner life; at the same time, it perceives calls coming from above.

In this laborious and painful evolution which involves all beings, there is a consoling fact upon which it is necessary to insist, namely that, at every stage of its ascent, the soul is attracted, aided, and rescued by higher-order entities. All spirits on the move are helped by their more advanced siblings and must in turn help those that are below them. Each individuality forms a link of the great chain of beings. The solidarity that unites them may restrict the freedom of each of them, but if this freedom is limited in its extent, it is not in its intensity. If the action of the chain link is limited, a single pulse coming from it can agitate the whole chain.

This constant fertilizing of the lower world by the higher world is a thing of wonder. All brilliant intuitions, deep inspirations and mighty revelations come thereof. In all eras, high thought has always radiated into the human brain. God, in Its equity, has never refused Its assistance or Its light to any nations or people. To all, It has sent guides, missionaries, prophets. The truth is one and it is eternal; it penetrates into humanity by means of successive radiations, as our understanding becomes more disposed to assimilate it.

Each new revelation is a continuation of an older one. This typifies Modern Spiritualism,[16] whose teachings bring a more complete knowledge of the role of every human being, a revelation of its hidden powers, and also of its inner relations with higher and divine thought.

Humans, as spirits incarnate, have forgotten their true role. Buried in the material world, they lost sight of the great horizons of their destiny, and disdained the means of developing their latent potentials, of making themselves happier by making themselves better. The new revelation (Spiritism) reminds us of all these things. It comes to shake

---

16 [Trans. note] *Neo-Spiritualism* and *New Spiritualism* are neologisms used interchangeably by Léon Denis to mean *Spiritism*.

slumbering souls, to stimulate their march, to induce their elevation. It illuminates the dark folds of the self, telling us about our origins and destinies, explaining the past through the present, and opening the prospects of a future that we are free to make magnificent or miserable according to our deeds.

―――

A human soul can only really progress by living in collective life, working for the benefit of all. One of the consequences of this solidarity which binds us so tightly is that the spectacle of the sufferings of some fellow beings disturbs and nullify serenity in others.

This is also a constant concern for Higher-order Spirits, which visit the dark regions, bringing the radiations of their thought and the impulsions of their love to the souls fallen in the paths of passion and error. No soul will forever be lost; if all of them have suffered, all will be saved. In the midst of their painful trials, the compassion and affection of their sibling souls will embrace them and lead them to God.

Indeed, how can we conceive that radiant spirits would forget those they once loved, those who shared their joys, their worries and are still struggling in the earthly paths? The complaint of those who are suffering, of those whom destiny still binds to backward worlds, comes to them and awakens their generous compassion. When one of these calls crosses the ether, those higher spirits leave their celestial dwellings to pour the treasures of their charitable love into the furrows of material worlds. Like light's vibrations, the impulsions of their love spread through the large expanse, bringing consolation to saddened hearts, pouring the balm of hope over the wounds of human beings.

Sometimes, during sleep too, drawn by their elder siblings, earthly souls rush forward to the heights of the spiritual plane for soaking up life-giving fluids from the eternal homeland. There, friendly spirits surround and exhort them, comforting them, and soothing their anguish. Then, they gradually extinguish the light around those souls, so that heart-wrenching regrets of that separation do not overwhelm them, and then carry them back to the frontiers of the lower worlds. Their awakening is melancholic but sweet; and, although they cannot remember their temporary stay in the high regions, they feel comforted and glad when they resume the toils of their daily life here below.

Among evolved souls, the feeling of solidarity becomes intense enough to change into perpetual communion with all beings and with God.

The pure soul communicates with the whole nature; it is inebriated with the infinite splendors of the Creator's works. The stars in the sky, the flowers in the meadow, the murmur of the running stream, the variety of earthly landscapes, the fleeting horizons of the sea, the serenity of deep space, absolutely everything speaks a harmonious language to it. In all these visible things, an attentive soul detects a manifestation of the invisible thought that animates the Cosmos. This is really striking for it. The Cosmos becomes the theater of universal life and communion, a communion of beings with one another, and all beings with God, their Parent.

No distance can separate akin souls from one another. Just as worlds exchange their radiations through the starry depths, so also those souls that love each other communicate together through thought. The universe is animated by a powerful life; it vibrates like a harp touched by divine strokes. The radiations of thought traverse it in all directions; they transmit messages from spirit to spirit throughout the vast expanse. This universe, which God has peopled with intelligences, so that they may know It, love It and fulfill Its law, while filling themselves with Its presence, and suffusing themselves with Its light warmed by Its endless love.

Prayer is the highest expression of communion of souls. Considered from this point of view, it loses all analogy with banal formulas, the monotonous formulas in use, to become a surge of the heart, an act of the will by which the spirit breaks away from the servitudes of matter and earthly coarseness to penetrate the laws, the mysteries of the infinite power, and submit to them in all things, without exception: "Ask, and it will be given to you." (Matthew 7:7) In this sense, prayer is the most important act of one's life; it is the ardent aspiration of the human being who feels his or her own smallness and misery, and seeks, if only for a moment, to put the vibrations of their thought in harmony with the eternal symphony. It is the work of meditation which, in recollection and silence, elevates the soul to these celestial heights where it increases its forces, where it impregnates itself with the radiations of divine light and love. Yet how few are able to pray! Religions have made us unlearn prayer by changing it into an idle exercise, sometimes quite simply ridiculous.

Under the influence of New Spiritualism (i.e., Spiritism), prayer will become more noble and worthy; it will be made with more respect for the supreme power; with more faith, confidence and sincerity; completely detached from material things. All our anxieties and uncertainties will cease when we come to understand that life is universal communion, and that God and all Its children live this life together. Then, prayer will become the language of all, the irradiation of the soul which, in its impulsions, sets in motion the spiritual and divine dynamism. Its benefits will extend to all beings and especially to those who suffer, the forgotten of the Earth and space. It will reach those whom no one dreams of benefiting, those who lie in the darkness, sadness and oblivion, in face of an accusing past. It will awaken in them new aspirations; it will strengthen their hearts and thoughts. For the range of prayer has no limits, any more than the forces and powers that it can conjure up for the good of others.

Prayer, it is true, are unable to change the immutable laws; it cannot modify our destinies in any way; its role is to provide us with help and enlightenment, making it easier to fulfill our earthly tasks. Fervent prayer opens wide the doors of the soul and, through these openings, force rays come in, radiations of the eternal core penetrate and vivify us.

To work with a lofty feeling, by pursuing a useful and generous goal, is still to pray. Work is the active prayer of millions of people who struggle and toil on Earth for the benefit of humanity.

The life of a good individual is a continual prayer, a perpetual communion with fellow beings and with God. Such individuals no longer need words or external formulas to their express faith: it is expressed by all their actions and thoughts. They breathe and move without effort in a pure fluidic atmosphere, full of tenderness toward the unfortunate, full of goodwill for all humanity. For these individuals, constant communion becomes a necessity, like a second nature. Thanks to it that all spirits of higher degree are kept at the sublime heights of inspiration and genius.

Those who lead a selfish and material life, whose comprehension is not open to influences from above, have no idea of the ineffable impressions that such communion with the divine can bring to one's soul.

It is this close union of our wills with the supreme Will, that must endeavor to support all those who, seeing the human species slide down into the slopes of moral decadence, look for ways to halt this fall. No ascension is possible, no actual drive for good, if we do not turn to our Creator and Parent from time to time, showing It our weaknesses, our uncertainties, our miseries, and asking It for spiritual help indispensable for our elevation. And the deeper this confession, the closer, more frequent, more sincere and profound our intimate communion with God becomes, improving and purifying our souls. Under the gaze of God, the soul examines, spreads its intentions, its feelings, its wishes; it reviews all its actions and, with that intuition that comes from above, it tells good from bad, what must be eliminated or else cultivated. It then realizes that everything that comes from the ego must be lowered to make room for self-denial, altruism; that in the sacrifice of oneself, the human being ultimately finds the most powerful means of elevation – for the more it gives of itself, the more it grows and flourishes. Self-sacrifice becomes the law of one's life, a law deeply imprinted in one's being in lines made of light, so that all of one's actions might become thus marked.

Standing on the ground which supports me and nurses me like a mother, I look up to the infinite above, feeling enveloped in the immense communion of life. The emanations of the Universal Soul penetrate me and make my thoughts and my heart vibrate. Powerful forces sustain me, bringing life to my existence. Wherever I lay my eyes, wherever my reasoning may lead me, I can see, discern, and contemplate the great harmony which governs all beings, and which guides them through several different means toward a unique and sublime goal. I see Goodness, Love, and Justice spreading out and radiating everywhere!

O God! My Creator! Source of all wisdom and love, Supreme Spirit whose name is Light, I lift my praises and aspirations unto you! May they rise to you like the scent of flowers, and climb to heaven like the inebriating fragrances of woods. Help me advance on the sacred path of knowledge to a higher understanding of your laws, so that my compassion and love for this great human family may increase. For I know that, only through my own moral perfectionment and the active fulfillment of charitable love and goodness applied around me to the benefit of all, I will eventually come closer to you, and become worthy of knowing you better, of communicating more intimately with you in the great harmony of beings and things. Help me freed myself from material life, help me understand and feel what is the higher, infinite life. Dispel any darkness that may envelop me; place in my soul a spark of that divine fire that warms and ignites the spirits of celestial spheres. May your sweet light and, with it, sentiments of concord and peace, spread over all beings!

IV

HARMONIES OF
THE SPHERES

One of the impressions that night enable us to observe in heaven is its majestic silence. Yet such silence is only apparent; it results from the limited perception of our organs. For higher evolved beings, gifted with senses open to the subtle sounds of the infinite, all the worlds vibrate, sing, pulsate, and together form an immense concert with their vibrations.

This law of great celestial harmonies can be observed in our own solar system.

We know that the order in which planets succeed each other in space is regulated by a law of progression, called Bode's law. Distances double from planet to planet, from the sun. Each group of planetary satellites obeys the same law. But this mode of progression has a principle and a meaning. This principle is related both to the laws of number and measure, to mathematics and to harmony.[17]

Planetary distances are set according to the regular order of harmonic progression; they express the very order of vibrations of each of these planets; and the planetary harmonies, calculated according to these rules, yield a perfect agreement. One could compare the solar system to an immense harp whose planets represent the strings. It would be possible, says Azbel, "by reducing to sound

---

[17] AZBEL (pseudonym of Émile-Abel CHIZAT), *Harmonie des Mondes* (Paris: Hughes Robert, 1903), *passim.*

strings the progression of planetary distances, to build up a complete and perfectly attuned instrument."[18]

Essentially – and therein lies the beauty of it – the law that governs the relations of sound, light and heat, is the same that governs the motion, the formation and the balance of spheres, at the same time setting their mutual distances. This law is the very same found in numbers, forms, and ideas. It is the law of harmony par excellence: it is the thought, a glimpse God's action!

Human language is very poor; it is insufficient to express the delightful mysteries of eternal harmony. Only musical composition can provide a suitable synthesis, and communicate its esthetic impression. Music, a divine language, expresses the rhythm of numbers, lines, shapes, movements. It is through it that the depths come alive and vibrate. It fills with its waves the colossal edifice of the universe, an august temple where the hymn of infinite life resounds.

Pythagoras and Plato already thought they could perceive "the music of the spheres." In the dream of Scipio, which Cicero recounts in one of the most beautiful pages bequeathed to us by Antiquity, the sleeper converses with the souls of his father Lucius Aemilius and his grandfather Scipio the African; he contemplates with them the celestial wonders and then the following dialogue is established:[19]

"And, as I gazed on these things with amazement, when I recovered myself: 'What,' I asked, 'what is this sound that fills my ears, so loud and sweet?' 'This,' he replied, 'is that sound, which divided in intervals, unequal, indeed, yet still exactly measured in their fixed proportion, is produced by the impetus and movement of the spheres themselves, and blending sharp tones with grave, therewith makes changing symphonies in unvarying harmony."

---

[18] *Op. cit.*, p. 29.

[19] [Trans. note] CICERO, *The Dream of Scipio Africanus Minor* (Trans. W. D. Pearman. Cambridge: Deighton, Bell & Co.,1883), p. 8.

Nearly all composers of genius who have been champions of the musical art, such as Bach, Beethoven, Mozart, and others, have said that they perceived harmonies far superior to all that can be conceived and that it was impossible for them to transcribe them. Beethoven, while composing, was beside himself, carried away in a sort of ecstasy, and writing feverishly, while vainly trying to reproduce that heavenly music which intoxicated him.

For one to be receptive to this degree, a remarkable psychical ability is needed. The very few humans that possess it say that all those who have grasped the musical sense of the universe have found this superior form, an ideal expression of eternal beauty and harmony. The highest conceptions of the human race are but a distant echo of it, a lessened vibration of the great symphony of the spheres.

It is the source of the purest joys of the Spirit, the secret of the higher life, which our dense senses still prevent us from understanding, from feeling its power and intensity. For those who can taste them fully, time has no more measure or limit, and the succession of countless days seems but a single day. Yet these still unsuspected joys will be provide by our evolution, as we ascend in the scale of existences and worlds.

Already we know of spirit mediums who can perceive sweet melodies, in a state of trance. Their abundant tears testify to the reality of their sensations.

~

Let us return to the study of the motion of the spheres and note that there is nothing – even when dealing with apparent exceptions to the universal law of harmony, and deviations of planets – that cannot be explained and even so cause admiration. There is a sort of "dialogue of vibrations as close as possible to unison,"[20] which is an additional esthetic charm of this wonder of beauty that we call the universe.[21]

One of the most striking examples is offered by the so-called telescopic planets,[22] which evolve between Mars and Jupiter, numbering more than twenty, occupying an entire octave space, divided into as many degrees; hence the probability that this set of worlds does not constitute, as we have thought, a universe of debris, but the laboratory of several worlds in formation, worlds that the study of space in future may point to a possible genesis.

The great harmonic relations which regulate the respective situations of each of the planets in our solar system are four in number, applied as follows:

Firstly, there is the one that goes from the Sun to Mercury; also at this point harmonious forces are at work; new planets are emerging.

Then, from Mercury to Mars, there is the region of the small planets, where our Earth moves; it plays a local dominant role, with a tendency of moving away from the sun to get closer to higher planetary harmonies. Mars, the component of this group whose continents we can see through the telescope, along with its seas, gigantic canals, and the whole apparatus of a civilization anterior to ours. Although smaller, Mars is better balanced than our planet.

Then come 500 telescopic planets (i.e., asteroids), which constitute a transitional interval; they form like a necklace of celestial pearls connecting the group of lower planets to the imposing chain of giant planets, from Jupiter to Neptune and beyond. This belt forms the fourth harmonic

---

20 [Trans. note] Uncredited quote of AZBEL (see footnote 17 above).
21 See supplemental note no. 3 at the end of this book.
22 [Trans. note] *Telescopic planets*, today called *asteroids*.

ratio, with decreasing notes like the volume of the giant spheres that compose it. In this group, Jupiter has the dominant role; the two modes, major and minor, are combined in it.[23]

"As in the harmonic inversion of sound," says Azbel,[24] "it is by a steady progression that the ancient group from Neptune to Jupiter asserts the formation of its volumes. The chaos of telescopic corpuscles, which follows, stopped this progression abruptly. Jupiter remained there, like a second sun, at the threshold of the two systems. From octave and second dominant roles, it has moved on to that of secondary and relative tonic, to express the character of the special role, obviously minor and relative, compared to that of the Sun, which it was going to fill, while young formations were disposed of on this side, gradually removing it and the worlds it now has under its guardianship from the celestial star of which it is the strongest offspring."

Strong indeed, Jupiter is very imposing in its orbit. I like to contemplate this colossal planet during calm summer nights, twelve hundred times bigger than our globe, escorted by its five satellites, of whose one, Ganymede, is as big as a planet. Standing on the plane of its orbit, so as to enjoy a perpetual equality of temperature in all latitudes, with days and nights always uniform in their duration, it is moreover composed of elements of our times less density than our massive home, which allows us to figure out, for the beings who live or will one say live in Jupiter, an ease of dislocation movement, potential for aerial life which would make it a station of predilection. What a magnificent

23 [Trans. note] Nowadays referred to as the Kuiper Belt. Note that Léon Denis's remarks are entirely based on the highly romanticized Az-BEL texts, who was a musical composer, not an astronomer or physicist.

24 AZBEL (pseudonym of Émile-Abel Chizat), *Harmonie des Mondes* (Paris: Hughes Robert, 1903), p. 13.

scenario for life! What a scene of enchantment and dream is conjured up by this giant orb!

Even more peculiar and wonderful is Saturn, whose appearance is so impressive through the telescope. Saturn, the equivalent of almost 9.5 Earths in size, with its huge ring-shaped diadem and eight satellites, among which Titan equals the size of Mars itself.

Saturn, with the rich procession that accompanies it in its slow orbit through space, constitutes in itself a veritable universe, a reduced image of the solar system. It is a world of work and thought, of science and art, where manifestations of intelligence and life develop in forms of unimaginable variety and richness. Its esthetic is a learned and complex one; in it the sense of beauty is made more subtle and deeper by the alternating movements, the eclipses of the satellites and rings, and all the play of light and shadow, of colors, where their shades melt into hues unknown the eyes of earthlings. Also harmonic chords, so moving in their analogy to those of the entire solar system!

Next, on the borders of the Sun's empire, Uranus and Neptune, both mysterious and magnificent planets, whose joint volume is nearly eight times bigger than the Earth. The harmonic note of Neptune would be: "the culminating of general agreement, the summit of the major agreement of the whole system" (Azbel). Then there are other distant planets, sentinels lost from our celestial group, still unnoticed, but guessed and even calculated, according to the influence they exert on the confines of our system, a long chain which links us to other families of worlds.

Further on lies the immense stellar ocean, a bottomless pit of light and harmony, whose melodious waves envelop all corners of the universe and cradle our solar system, a universe for us so vast, yet so puny compared to the Hereafter. It is the mysterious region of the unknown constantly drawing our thought, which is powerless to measure or define it, with its millions of suns of all sizes, of all potencies, these double stars, multiple orbs so colorful, scary cores that illuminate deep space, pouring out light, heat, and energy. At tremendous speeds they cover the immensity with their processions of worlds, invisible but guessed lands of the sky; and the human families that inhabit them, the peoples and their cities, the great civilizations of which they are the fulcrum.

Wonders and wonders are found everywhere succeeding one another: groups of suns animated with strange colors, archipelagos of stars; disheveled comets, wandering in the night, at their aphelions, dying cores that suddenly reignite and blaze at the bottom of the abyss; pale nebulae forming fantastic garlands, luminous ghosts whose radiations, Herschel[25] tells us, can take up to two million years to reach us. All these formidable geneses in the universe, cradles and tombs of universal life, voices from the past, promises of the future, are the splendors of infinity!

And all these worlds bring together their vibrations in a powerful melody. The soul, once delivered from earthly bonds and reaching these heights, can hear the deep voice of the eternal heavens!

~

As a whole, the harmonic relations which regulate the planetary distances represent exactly, as established by Azbel,[26] the extent of musical keyboards. Octave ratios,

25 [Trans. note] Frederick William HERSCHEL (1738–1822), discoverer of Uranus, was the elder member of an illustrious family of German-British astronomers.

26 AZBEL (pseudonym of musician Émile-Abel Chizat), *Harmonie des Mondes* (Paris: Hughes Robert, 1903), p. 10.

or harmonic powers, are identical to those of distances and the law of movements. Our solar system represents a kind of eight-story building, that is to say, eight octaves, with a staircase of 320 steps or harmonic waves, on which the planets are placed, occupying "levels indicated by the harmony of a perfect multiple chord."

Dissonances are only apparent or transient. Agreement is at the bottom of everything. The rules of our musical harmony seem to be only a consequence, a very imperfect application of the law of sovereign harmony which presides over the march of the worlds. We can therefore logically believe that the melodic harmony of the spheres would be intelligible to our spirit, if our senses could perceive the sound waves that fill deep space.[27]

However, for being absolute, the general rule is not narrow and rigid. In some cases, as in planet Neptune's, relative harmony seems to depart from the principle, although never really coming out of it. The study of planetary movements provides an obvious demonstration of this occurrence.

In this order of studies, more than in any other, we see manifest in its imposing grandeur the law of Beauty and Perfection which governs the whole universe. No sooner is our attention turned toward the sidereal immensities, than immediately our sense of esthetics becomes intense. This sense will grow even more and be heightened as the

---

[27] "Mr. Émile Chizat," says AZBEL (in *la Musique dans l'espace*), finds that so-called "celestial voices" when playing the organ is nothing else than the intuitive musical application of the important role of "ideas from the stars." It is likely that symphonic creations will appear later exploring this subject, which could leave the public with unexpected impressions. May they at least help reduce our "earthly" music, which is lost, raising it to notions a little higher and more representative of a priesthood of harmony which they ought to fulfill among us. [Trans. note: AZBEL was the pseudonym of Émile Chizat, who therefore was referring to no other but himself in this excerpt.]

rules of universal harmony become clearer, as the veil that hides celestial splendors from us is raised.

Everywhere, we will find this harmonic agreement which enchants and moves us. In this domain, there are none of these discordances, these disappointments so frequent in the heart of humanity. Everywhere this power of beauty unfolds, bringing its combinations to infinity, embracing in one same whole all the laws, in every sense: arithmetic, geometry, esthetics.[28]

The universe is a sublime poem of which we are just beginning to spell the first verses. We can only catch a few notes, some distant and weak murmurs, and already these first notes of the marvelous musical alphabet fill us with enthusiasm. What will it be then, when, once we become more worthy of interpreting the divine language, we start to perceive and understand the great harmonies of space, the infinite agreement in their infinite variety, the song sung by those millions of stars which, in the prodigious diversity of their volumes and movements, give out vibrations for an eternal symphony?

But after all – one may ask – such heavenly music, such voice from deep space, what is it saying?

This rhythmic language is the Word par excellence, the one by which all the worlds and higher beings communicate with one another, calling each other through the distances; and through which we too will communicate one day with other human families that populate the starry space.

At the very core of vibrations used in the translation of thought, lies universal telegraphy, the vehicle of ideas conveyed throughout all regions of the universe, by which

---

28 "In harmonic calculations," says AZBEL in *Harmonie des Mondes*, p. 80, "the sense of quantity, the Number, is always enlightened and completed by the meaning of the musical note, that is, by the meaning of the harmonic quality that such number contains." [Trans. note: *Cf.* Léon DENIS, *Spiritism in the Arts*, New York: USSF, 2018.]

elevated souls carry out perpetual exchanges and outpour-
ings of science, wisdom and love, talking from one star to
another about their common works, goals to be achieved,
progress to be made.

It is also the hymn sang to God by the worlds, alternately
a song of joy, adoration, complaint, and prayer; it is the
great voice of the spheres, the supreme harmony of beings
and things, the cry of love that goes up eternally to the
ordering Intelligence of the many universes.

When will we be able to detach our thoughts from
everyday banalities and bring them up to these heights?
When will we be able to penetrate these mysteries of space
and understand that each discovery made, each conquest
pursued in this path of light and beauty, contributes to
ennoble our spirits, to heighten our moral life, and to give
us joys superior to all those of material world?

When will we finally understand that it is there, in this
splendid universe, that our own destiny unfolds, and that
to study it is to study the very environment in which we
are called to live again and again, to evolve ceaselessly,
suffusing ourselves more and more with the harmonies that
fill the immensity of space? That everywhere life blossoms
into blooms of souls? That space is populated by countless
civilizations to which human beings are bonded through
the laws of their own nature and future?

Ah, how pitiful are those who turn their eyes away
from this spectacle, and their spirits from these problems!
Because there is no study more impressive or more moving,
no higher revelation in science or art, no more sublime a
lesson to be learned.

No, the secret of our happiness, our power, our future,
is not in the ephemeral things of this world, but rather in
the teachings from above and beyond. And human teachers
and educators turn out to be very unconscious or guilty,

when they neglect teaching souls toward the heights where the true light shines.

If doubt and uncertainty besiege us, if life seems too heavy to bear, if we grope in the dark of night in search of a purpose, if pessimism and sadness invade us, then we only have ourselves to blame, for the great infinite book remains there, open before our eyes, with its magnificent pages, each word a group of stars, each letter a sun – the big book in which we must learn to read the sublime teachings. Truth is there, written in flaming gold letters; it beckons to us, inviting our gaze: Truth, a reality far more beautiful than all legends and fictions put together.

It is truth which tells us of the imperishable life of the soul, which reincarnates and lives on the spiral of worlds innumerable stages on a radiant path, pursuing the eternal good in the infinite duration, the climbing of heavens toward the conquest of full awareness and conscience, the joy of living forever to love, to always ascend, to always acquire new powers, higher virtues, wider perceptions. And above all, vision, understanding, the possession of eternal beauty, the bliss of penetrating its laws, of associating more closely with the divine work and the evolution of civilizations.

Because of these magnificent studies, the idea of God emerges even more majestic and serene. The science of celestial harmonies is like a grand pedestal upon which the awe-inspiring figure of sovereign beauty stands, whose shining brightness, too dazzling for our feeble eyes, remains veiled, but radiates gently through the obscurity that envelopes it.

Idea of God, the ineffable center toward which all the sciences, all the arts, all the higher truths converge and blend into a boundless synthesis. Idea which is the first and the last word of present or past things, near or far away; the Law itself, the sole cause of all causes, the absolute, fundamental unity of Good and Beauty, which thought requires, which conscience demands; and in which the human soul finds its reason for being and the inexhaustible source of its forces, lights, and inspirations!

V

NECESSITY FOR
THE IDEA OF GOD

In the preceding chapters I have endeavored to demonstrate the necessity of the idea of God. It asserts itself and imposes itself outside and above all systems, all philosophies, all beliefs. It is therefore free from all attachment to any religion that we proceed in this study, with absolute independence of thought and conscience. For God is greater than all theories and systems. This is why it cannot be affected or diminished by the mistakes and flaws that humans have made in Its name. God hovers above everything.

God is above all denominations, and if we call It God, it is for want of a greater name, as Victor Hugo once said.

The question of God is the most serious of all the issues hanging over our heads, the solution of which is narrowly connected in an imperious way to the problem of human beings and their destinies, to the problem of individual life versus social life.

Knowledge of the truth about God, about the world and life is the most essential and necessary, because such knowledge sustains us, inspires us, and give us a direction, even when we are unaware of its importance. Besides, this truth is not inaccessible, as we shall see below; it is simple and clear; it is within the reach of each and every one. All one has to do is to look for it without prejudice, without bias, using conscience and reason.

I will not mention here all the theories and innumerable systems that religions and philosophical schools have raised throughout the centuries. Few of us today give any importance to their disputes, their anger, and their vain agitations buried in the past.

To elucidate such a subject, we now have higher resources than those of human thought; we have the teaching of those who have left the Earth, the appreciation of souls that, having crossed the tomb, make us hear from the heart of the unseen world, their opinions, their calls, and their exhortations.

It is true that not every spirits is equally prepared for dealing with these issues. There are spirits from beyond the grave which are just like average humans. Spirits are not all equally developed; not all of them have reached the same degree of evolution. Hence, some contradictions and differences in their viewpoints. However, above the mass of obscure, ignorant, backward souls, there are eminent spirits, which descend from the high spheres to enlighten and guide humanity.

So what do they have to say about the question of God?

The existence of a supreme Power is unanimously affirmed by all higher-order spirits. Those of us who have studied philosophical Spiritism know that all great spirits, whose teachings have comforted our souls, soothed our miseries, and sustained us throughout our failures, have consistently asserted, proclaimed, and acknowledged that a high Intelligence governs all beings and worlds. They say that this Intelligence becomes more vivid and sublime as one ascends the degrees of spiritual life. The same is true of Spiritist writers and philosophers, from Allan Kardec to those of the present day: All affirm the existence of an eternal, universal cause.

"There is no effect without a cause," said Kardec in *The Spirits' Book*. "Every intelligent effect must have an intelligent cause." This is the basic principle upon which all Spiritism rests. This principle, when applied to manifestations from beyond the grave, demonstrates the existence of spirits. When applied to the study of the world and universal laws, it demonstrates the existence of an intelligent cause in the universe. That is why the existence of God is one of the essential points of Spiritist teachings. Further, I could add that it is inseparable from the rest of its teachings, because in the latter everything is connected, coordinated, and linked. Do not mention dogmas! Spiritism is devoid of any. It imposes nothing; it just teaches. All teaching has its principles. The idea of God is one of the fundamental principles of Spiritism.

At times, some people have told me: "What good is it to deal with this question of God? The existence of God cannot be proved!" Or again: "The existence or non-existence of God has no impact whatsoever in the life of the populace, let alone in the whole humanity. Let us deal with something more practical; let us not waste our time in vain dissertations and metaphysical discussions."

Well, though I mean no offense to those who hold such opinions, I would like to stress once again that the question of God remains the supreme question, the vital question par excellence; I should also add that humans cannot lose interest in the subject, because humans are beings. As human beings we live, and it is important for us to know what is the source, the cause, what is the law of life. The opinion one has of the cause, of the law of the universe, this opinion, whether one likes it or not, whether one knows it or not, is reflected in one's actions, in one's whole life, whether publicly or privately.

Whatever our ignorance of the higher laws, in reality it is from our notion of these laws, vague and confusing as it may be, and according to them, that we humans have been acting. It is based on their opinion of God, the world, and life – note that these three subjects are inseparable – that human societies live or perish!

It is this opinion that divides humanity into two camps. And everywhere we see families in conflict, in intellectual dissension, because there are several systems about God: the priest having instilled one of them into a family member; the professor having taught a different system to another member of the same family, when not altogether suggesting the idea of nothingness to the student.

Moreover, these disputes and contradictions can be perfectly explained. They have a reason to exist. Bear in mind that not all spirits have reached the same evolutionary level; not everyone can see and understand in the same way and in every sense. Hence so many clashing views, different beliefs. The ability that we have of understanding, of judging, of discerning, only slowly develops in us from century to century, from lifetime to lifetime. Our knowledge, our understanding of things, achieves completion and enlightenment as we rise on the immense ladder of rebirths. Everybody knows it: the one that is placed at the foot of a mountain cannot see what unfolds to the other who has reached the summit. But as we continue to climb, we too eventually see the same things as the others. The same happens to the spirit in its gradual ascension. The universe is revealed to us only gradually, as our ability to understand its laws grows exponentially.

Hence the systems, the philosophical and religious schools which respond to varying degrees of development of spirits which identify themselves with them, often confining themselves to them.

VI

UNIVERSAL LAWS

Let me repeat that all scientific works accomplished since the mid-19th century show us the existence and action of natural laws. These laws are connected by a higher law which encompasses them all, regulating them and bringing them back to unity, order, and harmony. It is through these wise and profound laws, the organizers which give order to the universe, that the supreme Intelligence is revealed.

Truly, some scholars object that universal laws are blind. But how can blind laws guide the march of the worlds in space, regulate all the phenomena, all the manifestations of life, and do all that with admirable precision? If laws are blind, it may be inferred they act necessarily at random. But chance would be a lack of direction, the absence of any acting intelligence. Any such concept would be irreconcilable with the notion of order and harmony.

In my view, the idea of law seems therefore inseparable from the idea of intelligence. A law is the manifestation of an intelligence, because it is the work of thought. Only it could have been able to organize and arrange all things in the universe. And thought cannot occur without the existence of a being which is its generator.

There can be no law extraneous to and without the help of intelligence, of a will that directs it. Otherwise law would indeed be blind, as materialists say, but then it would be left to chance, to variable drifting. It would be exactly as if a someone wanting to follow a road without the help of sight and thus falling into a ditch after a few

steps. Therefore it can be said that a law that is blind would
no longer be a law.

We have just seen that researches conducted by science
demonstrate the existence of universal laws. Every day
science advances often without being aware of it, but ultimately it advances little by little toward that great unity
which we detect at the bottom of things.

We have just seen that researches conducted by science
demonstrate the existence of universal laws. Every day
science advances often without being aware of it, but ultimately it advances little by little toward that great unity
which we perceive at the bottom of things.

Not even positivists and materialists can avoid to be
drawn by this movement of ideas. They proceed, without
noticing it, toward this magnificent conception which unites
all the forces and laws of the universe. Indeed, it could be
established that Auguste Comte, Littré, Robinet, and the
whole positivist school, have approached these issues with
the most flagrant contradictions. They reject the idea of
the absolute, that is, the idea of a generative cause, and
instead proclaim and even claim to prove that "matter is
only the sensible manifestation of a universal principle."
According to them, "all sciences superimpose themselves and
ultimately unite in a supreme generality which seals their
unity." Paraphrasing Emile Burnouf, "Science is about to
come up with a theory, whose general formula will establish
a correlation between all substance and the invariability of
life, and their indissoluble unity with thought."[29]

Now, what exactly is this triad of substance, life and
thought, this "supreme generality," this "universal law,"
this "unique principle," which presides over all phenomena
of Nature, all metamorphoses, all the acts of life, all the

---

[29] [Trans. note] Cf. E. BURNOUF, *The Science of Religions* (Trans. J.
Liebe. London: Swan Sonnenschein, Lowrey & Co., 1888), pp. 274–275.
BURNOUF's extensive text is not quoted but summarized above.

inspirations of the spirit? After all, what is this central point to which all there is, all that lives, all that thinks converge, sum up and coalesce? What, if not the absolute, if not God Itself!

It is true that the more one denies the attributes of intelligence and consciousness to the absolute, to the cause supreme, the more one will spend time trying to explain how an unintelligent, blind and unconscious cause could be able to produce all the magnificent formations of the cosmos, all the splendors of intelligence, of light and life without ever knowing what it was doing. How, without any consciousness or will, any thought or judgment, could it have produced beings that think, wish, and judge, and that are endowed with conscience and reason?

Everything comes from and returns to God. A fluid more subtle than the ether emanates from the Creator's thought. As a result of successive combinations, this fluid – exceedingly quintessential to be grasped by our understanding – has become the ether. From the ether have come all the graded forms of matter and life. Once arriving at the final point of descent, substance and life then trace back the immense cycle of evolution.

As we have seen, the orderly majesty of the universe is not revealed only through the movement of stars, or in the march of the worlds. It also reveal itself, in a most imposing way, in the evolution and development of life on the surface of these worlds. Today, we can establish that life develops, transforms and refines itself following a preconceived plan; and perfects itself as it goes through its immense path. We are beginning to understand that everything is set for a goal, and that goal is the evolution of all beings; the continual increase and realization in one's being of ever more perfect forms of beauty, wisdom, and moral principles.

All around us, we can observe this majestic law of progress operating through the slow work of Nature: from the lowest forms and infinitely small protozoans floating in water, to higher species, rising step by step on the scale until it reaches the human level. Then instinct becomes sensibility, intelligence, consciousness, and reason. We also know that this climb will not stop there. Through the teachings of the Hereafter, we learn that it goes on and on in the unseen worlds, through increasingly subtle forms. It continues from power to power, from glory to glory until it reaches infinity, even God. And this magnificent ascension of life can only be explained by the existence of a will, of an intelligent cause of inextinguishable energy, which penetrates and envelops all nature: it is it that regulates and stimulates this colossal evolution of life toward Good, Beauty and Perfection!

The same happens in the moral field. Our existences succeed one another and take place through the centuries. Events follow each other without us being aware that they are all linked. However an immanent justice hovers over all things. It sets our fate according to a law, according to an infallible principle. Thoughts, words, actions, everything is linked together, everything is connected by a series of causes and effects which are like the woof of our destinies.[30]

Let me insist upon one point: It is thanks to the revelation made by the spirits that the Law of Justice has been unveiled to us in all its majesty, its vast consequences, and the prodigious series of linked events dominated and governed by it.

30 See Léon DENIS. *The Problem of Life & Destiny* (Trans. H. M. Monteiro. New York: USSF, 2018), *passim*.

When you study the problem of future life, and examine the situation of the spirit after death – note that this remains the most important goal of psychical research – you find yourself in the presence of a considerable fact with a great deal of moral consequences. There is a state of affairs which is regulated by a law of balance and harmony.

As soon as the soul crosses the gates of physical death, as soon as it awakens in the homeland of spirits, the full picture of its past lifetimes unfolds little by little before its eyes. In it there is a mirror that faithfully reflects all the actions and deeds, to accuse or glorify the soul. No distraction, no escape is possible. The spirit is obliged to contemplate itself, firstly to recognize itself or to suffer, and later to prepare itself for another lifetime of progress or atonement. Hence, for the great majority of us, the regrets, shame and suffering!

The teachings from beyond the grave tell us that nothing is lost, whether good or evil, but rather everything is recorded, atoned for, and redeemed through new earthly existences, ever more difficult and painful.

We also learn that no effort is lost and that no suffering is in vain. Duty is not an empty word, and Good reigns unchallenged above everyone and everything. Each of us builds day by day, every hour, often without knowing it, our own future. The fate we endure in our current life has been prepared by our previous actions. Likewise, we are building in the present the conditions of our future existence. Hence, for the wise, resignation to what is inevitable in the current life; also a powerful encouragement for action, so as to devote oneself and prepare a better destiny.

Will those are aware of this be filled with fear when thinking of what awaits them in current society, whose thoughts, tendencies, and actions are too often inspired by selfishness or bad passions? This society that builds up above itself dark clouds of heavy spiritual fluids which carry a storm in their flanks?

How could one not be frightened in presence of so many moral failings, in face of so much corruption displayed everywhere, and realizing that the sentiment of good occupies so little room in certain consciences? Also afraid of finding in the depths of so many human souls, depression, demoralization, discouragement, and a disgust for life?

And if we feel that way, how could we hesitate to affirm to all others and make known to them this law of justice that the teachings of the Hereafter have shown us to be so huge, so imposing; this independent law that runs of itself, without any tribunal or judgment, but from which none of our actions can escape; a law which reveals a guiding intelligence of a moral world; a living law, conscious reason of the universe, the source of all life, of all light, and of all perfection!

That is what God is. The day this idea of God penetrates learning – and hence our minds and consciences – we will be able to understand that the principle of justice is nothing but an admirable instrument by which the supreme Cause brings everything back to order and harmony. And, finally, it will be felt that the idea of God is indispensable to modern societies, which have collapsed and perished morally because, by no longer understanding God, they become unable to regenerate themselves. Then all thoughts, all consciences, will turn to this moral core, to that source of eternal justice which is God, and we will see the face of the world completely change!

Justice is not only of social origin, like the French Revolution of 1789 tried to establish. It comes from higher; it is of divine origin. If humans stand equal before human law, it is because they have always been equal before the eternal law.

And it is also because we all come from the same source of intelligence and awareness that we are all fellow human beings, in solidarity with one another, and united in our immortal destinies. For solidarity and fraternity of all beings are only possible if they all feel connected to the same common core. We are children of the same Parent, because the human soul is an emanation of the divine soul, a spark of the eternal thought.

———

Everything, both visible and invisible, speaks of God. The intellect discerns It; reason and conscience proclaim It.

But the human being is not only reason and conscience; it is also love. What characterizes humans, above all else, is feeling, it is the heart. Feeling is a privilege of the soul; it is through this means that the human being is attached to everything that is good, beautiful and grand, and to all that deserves its confidence and can offer support when in doubt, its comfort in misfortune. Now, all these modes of feeling and conceiving also reveal the existence of God to us, for goodness, beauty and truth are found in the human being only in a partial, limited and incomplete state. Goodness, beauty, truth can exist only on the condition of recovering their principle, their fullness, their source within a being which possesses them in the highest state, in the infinite state.

The idea of God imposes itself upon us through all the faculties of our spirit, at the same time that it speaks to our eyes through all the splendors of the universe. The supreme intelligence is revealed as being the eternal cause, where all beings draw strength, light and life. This is the divine

Spirit, the powerful Spirit that is honored under so many different names, but which, under all these names, is always the core, the living law, the reason by which all beings and worlds feel alive, by which they know one another, renew and elevate themselves.

God speaks to us through all the voices of the infinite. It speaks to us, not through a Bible written centuries ago, but in a Bible that is written every day, through these majestic characters called the ocean, the seas, the mountains, the stars from the sky; and by all the sweet and deep harmonies rising from the bosom of the Earth or descending from ethereal spaces. God still speaks to us in the inner sanctum of our being, in the hours of silence and meditation. When the discordant noises of material life are silenced, then our inner voice, the great voice awakens and is heard. This voice comes out of the depths of consciousness and speaks of duty, progress, ascension. There is in us an intimate retreat, like a deep source from which streams of life, love, virtue, and light can flow. Therein this reflection, this divine seed hidden in every human soul, is fully manifested.

That is why the human soul is the most beautiful testimony that stands in favor of the existence of God: it is a radiance of the divine soul, it contains in embryonic state all the powers; its role, its destiny being to highlight them during the soul's innumerable lives, during its transmigrations through eras and worlds.

The human being, endowed with reason, is accountable; it is likely to know itself, and has the duty to govern itself. As John the Evangelist said: "The true light, which enlightens everyone, [has come] into the world." (John 1:9) Human reason, as we have said, is a spark of divine reason. It is by going back to its source, by communing with the absolute, eternal Reason, that it discovers the truth and understands the universal law and order. So I say to all, O fellow human beings! Children of the Light, O siblings of mine! Let us remember our origin; remember our true purpose during the journey of life! Let us detach ourselves from things that pass away; let us attach ourselves to things that last forever.

There are not two principles in the world, namely, good and evil. Evil is only a contrast effect, what night is for daylight. Darkness does not have its own existence. Evil is the state of inferiority and ignorance of one's being still in evolution. The first steps of the immense ladder represent what may be called evil; but as the being climbs up, it realizes the good in and around itself. On the other hand, pain subsides and fades. Evil, as has been said, is only the absence of good. If it seems to still dominate our planet, it is because Earth is one of the first rings of the chain, a stage for elementary souls which only just begun started the rough path of knowledge; or of guilty souls, still in the process of atonement. On more advanced worlds, good flourishes and, from degree to degree, ends up reigning absolutely.

As for Good, it is indefinable by itself. Defining it would be diminishing it. It must be considered, not in its nature, but through its manifestations.

Above all essences, forms, and ideas, hangs the principle of Beauty and Good, the highest degree achievable by us through thought, although still unable to fully embrace it. It is due to our infirmity that we are unable to grasp the ultimate reality of things; yet sensitivity, intelligence, and knowledge represent in us several points of support, which allow the soul to free itself from its state of inferiority and uncertainty, and to convince itself that everything in the universe, its forces and beings, absolutely everything is governed by Good and Beauty. The orderly majesty of the world, both physically and morally, justice, liberty, morality, everything rests on eternal laws, and there can be no eternal laws without a higher Principle, without a primary Reason, first cause of all laws. Therefore, the human being, let alone society, cannot grow and progress without the idea of God, that is: without justice, without freedom, without respect for oneself, without love; because God, representing perfection, is the last word, the supreme guarantee of all that constitutes beauty, the magnificence of life, in short, of everything that makes up the power and harmony of the universe!

VII

THE IDEA OF GOD
VERSUS PSYCHICAL
EXPERIMENTATION

So far in this study of the question of God, I have stood
on the ground of principles. In this field, the idea of
God appears as the keystone of Spiritualist tenets.
Let us now see whether it retains equal importance in the
field of facts, as established by psychical experiments.[31]

At first glance, it may sound strange to hear that the idea
of God would play a useful role in experimental studies, in
the observation of spiritual facts. Let me first remark that
there is a tendency on the part of certain groups to give
Spiritism a character above all experimental, attaching it
exclusively to the study of phenomena, while neglecting
its philosophical character; in short, a tendency to reject
anything that might recall, even in the least, philosophical
systems of the past, instead confining it solely to the scientific
field. In these circles, they deem it desirable to exclude the
belief and affirmation of God, considering it superfluous,
or at least impossible to demonstrate. This is supposedly
to attract scientists, positivists, freethinkers, and all those
who have a kind of aversion to any religious sentiment, to
anything having mystical or philosophical leanings.

On the other hand, there are those who would like to
make Spiritism a philosophical and moral teaching, based
on facts, a teaching capable of replacing old religions,

---

[31] See supplemental notes nos. 4, 5 and 6, at the end of this book.

obsolete systems, and of satisfying the many souls who seek, above all, comfort for their pains, a simple and popular philosophy, which give them some solace from the cares and sorrows of life.

On one side or the other, there are crowds to be satisfied; much more so on one side than the other, since the crowd of those who struggle and suffer is exceedingly larger than that formed by scholars and scientists.

To support these two theses, we see on both sides sincere individuals who are perfectly satisfied with their convictions, to whose qualities we like to pay homage. Who should we opt for? In what direction would it be appropriate to steer Spiritism so as to ensure its evolution? The result of my researches and observations have led me to recognize that the greatness of Spiritism, the influence it has acquired over the masses, comes especially from its tenets; the facts are only the foundations on which this building is based. There can be no doubt whatsoever that foundations play an essential role in any building, but it is not in the foundations, that is to say, in the underground structures, that thought and consciousness can find any shelter.

In my view, the real mission of Spiritism is not merely to enlighten the intellect by providing a more accurate and complete knowledge of the physical laws that rule the world; above all, it consists in developing the moral aspect of human life, a moral life which materialism and sensualism have greatly diminished. To elevate human nature and character, and to strengthen individual consciences, these are the paramount tasks of Spiritism. From this standpoint, it can be an effective remedy for all the evils that besiege contemporary society; a panacea for the incredible growth of selfishness and impetuous passions that have been pushing us into the abyss.

At this point, I think it is high time to state my entire conviction that, it is neither by turning Spiritism into an exclusively positive, experimental science, nor by eliminating everything of a higher nature in it – that is, anything that can raise our thoughts high above narrow horizons, into other words, upon the idea of God and the use of prayer – that we will facilitate Spiritism's main mission. On the contrary, such limitation would only render it sterile and ineffective in bringing progress to the masses.

There can also be no doubt of the great conquests of science; I myself have always done justice to the courageous efforts of scientists who make the limits of the unknown recede every day. But science does not encompass everything. Although it has certainly helped to enlighten humanity, it has also proved powerless to make it happier and better.

The greatness of the human spirit does not consist only in knowledge; it is also in one's high ideal. It was not science, but sentiment, faith and enthusiasm that made Joan of Arc, the French Revolution, and all the great sagas of history.

The envoys from above, the great predestined ones, the seers, the prophets, did not choose science as their motive; they chose belief. They did not hit brains; they touched hearts. All of them came to push the nations toward God.

What has become of the science of the past? Waves of oblivion have submerged it, as they will submerge today's science. What will be the methods used, the theories current in twenty centuries? Conversely, the names of the great missionaries have survived the test of time. What has survived everything in the disaster of civilizations is that which elevates the human soul above itself, toward a sublime goal, toward God!

And there is still something else. Even when confining ourselves to the field of experimental studies, there is one detail of capital importance that should always inspire us, namely, the nature of the relations which are established between humans and the world of the spirits: the study of conditions to be met in order to derive the best possible results from such rapports.

No sooner we approach these phenomena, we are struck by the composition of the invisible world which surrounds us, by the character of that multitude of spirits that envelop us, constantly seeking to put themselves in touch with incarnate humans. Around our backward planet hovers a powerful invisible life, where irresponsible and mocking spirits predominate, mixed with perverse and evil spirits. There are those controlled by passions or appetites, all kinds of vices and crimes. They have left the Earth with their souls full of hatred, their thoughts distorted by vengeance and scorn. They wait in the shadows for a propitious moment to satisfy their grudge and fury, at the expense of imprudent and incautious experimenters who, without any precaution or reserve, open wide the paths that make our world communicate with the spirits.

It is from this milieu that comes countless mystifications, audacious deceits, all sorts of maneuvers well known by experienced Spiritists, treacherous maneuvers, which in certain cases may lead spirit mediums to obsession, or even possession, and the loss of their finest faculties. So much so that some critics, in enumerating the victims of these facts, and listing all the abuses that derive from an inconsiderate and frivolous practice of Spiritism, end up wondering whether such practices are a source of danger and misery, and a new cause of decadence for humanity.[32]

---

[32] See J. MAXWELL, *Metapsychical Phenomena* (Trans. L. I. Finch, London: Duckworth & Co. 1905), pp. 384, 386; and Léon DENIS, *Into the Unseen* (Trans. H. M. Monteiro. New York: USSF, 2017), ch. XXII. See also *Compte rendu du Congrès Spirite de Bruxelles*, 1910, pp. 112, 121.

Fortunately, remedy is near the evil. To deliver us from bad influences, there is a supreme resource. We have a powerful means to ward off spirits from the abyss and to make Spiritism an element of regeneration, support and comfort. This resource, this support, is prayer, our thought directed toward God! The thought of God is like a light that dispels all shadows and drives away the spirits of darkness; it is a weapon that expels evil spirits and protects us from their pitfalls. Prayer, when it is ardent and spontaneous, instead of a monotonous recitation, has considerable dynamic and magnetic power;[33] it attracts higher-order spirits and ensures their protection. Thanks to them, we can thus communicate with those whom we have loved on Earth, those who have been flesh of our flesh, blood of our blood and who, from the heart of the spiritual world, stretch out their arms toward us.

I have seen this happen many times throughout my long experience as an experimenter: when, during a Spiritist meeting, all thoughts and wills are united in a powerful surge full of deep assurance, rising to God through prayer, Its help is never lacking. All these united wills constitute a bundle of forces, a sure weapon against evil. To the pleas that rise to heaven, there is always some spirit of higher degree ready to respond. This protective spirit, summoned from above, comes to direct our labors, to ward off lower-order spirits – it only allows spirits whose manifestations are useful for themselves or for us, incarnate humans.

There is an infallible principle in all this. With purified thought and elevation toward God, experimental Spiritism can become a source of light, a moral force, a giver of comfort. Without them, it becomes uncertain, a door open

---

33 I obtained positive proof by means of photographic plates. When praying, I succeeded in imprinting the plates by the contact of my fingers, with much more active radiations and more intense emanations than in my normal state.

to all traps and pitfalls of the unseen. It offers an open rift to all the influences, all the snares of the abyss, breaths of hatred, storms of evil, which pass over humanity like whirlwinds, filling it with disorder and ruin.

Indeed it is good, it is necessary to open roads to communicate with the spiritual world, but above all we should avoid that these roads are then used by our enemies to invade us. Let us remember that in the unseen world there are many impure elements. To open a rift to them would be to pour out innumerable evils into Earth: it would be the same as handing over to evil spirits a crowd of weak and disarmed souls. To enter into relations with the higher forces, with the enlightened spirits, one needs to bring together will and faith, an absolute selflessness, and elevation of thought. When neglecting these conditions, the experimenter becomes the plaything of irresponsible spirits. "Birds of a feather flock together," says the old proverb. In fact, the law of affinities governs the world of souls the same as it does with that of bodies.

Therefore there is a necessity, from a theoretical as well as practical standpoint, a necessity from the standpoint of Spiritism's progress, to develop our moral sense, to attach ourselves to strong beliefs, to higher principles, a necessity of not overdoing evocations, of contacting spirits only when we meet conditions of inner retreat and moral peace.

Spiritism has been given to humankind as a means of enlightening themselves, of improving themselves, of acquiring the qualities indispensable for their evolution. If anyone would destroy in souls or merely neglect the idea of God and high aspirations, Spiritism might then become a dangerous thing. This is why I do not hesitate to say that, to engage in Spiritist practices without first purifying your thoughts, without fortifying them with faith and prayer, you would be perpetrating a fatal deed, the responsibility of which would fall heavily on the culprits' shoulders.

~~~

Now there is a particularly delicate point that should also be addressed. Spiritists are sometimes reproached for not always living in harmony with their principles; they are told that, in them, sensualism, material appetites, love of financial gain, often occupy a considerable place in their lives. Spiritists are reproached above all for their internal divisions, the rivalries of groups and individuals, which pose a great obstacle to the organization of the Spiritist forces and to their advance.

It is not convenient for me to insist on these details here; I do not want to pass any unfavorable judgment on anybody. Let me just point out that it would not be by reducing Spiritism to a mere science of observation that one could succeed in mitigating and lessening these weaknesses. On the contrary, it would only make them worse. If exclusively experimental, Spiritism would no longer have the authority or moral strength necessary to connect souls. Some believe that the erasure of the idea of God would be beneficial to Spiritism. I would say that it is the current insufficiency of this notion of God and, at the same time, the insufficiency of noble sentiments and high aspirations, that have been responsible for the lack of cohesion and difficulties of organization in the Spiritist Movement. One thing must indeed be highlighted: as soon as the idea of God is weakened in one's soul, the notion of the ego, that is to say, of one's personality, grows up exponentially. It grows up to the point of becoming tyrannical and self-absorbing.

One of these notions can only grow and strengthen to the detriment of the other. One who does not worship God, said a thinker, actually worships oneself!

Whatever is good for Spiritist experimentation circles is also good for the whole society. As shown above, the idea of God is closely linked to the idea of law, as well as to the idea of duty and self-sacrifice. The idea of God is related to all the notions indispensable to order, to harmony, to the elevation of beings and societies. That is why, when the idea of God collapses, all these other notions enfeeble, vanishing little by little, and making way for selfish personalism, arrogant presumption, and for the hatred of all authority, of all direction, and of all higher law. And so, gradually, step by step, we arrive at this social situation, which can be summarized by that famous motto, a motto which I have often heard from all sides: *Neither God nor Master!*[34]

The idea of God has been so much abused over the centuries; distorted, with so many innocent victims sacrificed in its name; that in the name of God, the world has been soaked with human blood, to the point that modern humans have turned away from the Divinity. We are afraid that the responsibility for this state of affairs will fall on those who have turned the true God of goodness and eternal mercy into a God of vengeance and terror. But it is not up to us to establish accountabilities. Our goal is rather to seek a ground of conciliation and rapprochement where all good spirits can meet.

Be that as it may, modern humans for the most part do not wish to endure above them either God, law, or constraint any longer; they no longer want to hear that freedom without wisdom and without reason is impracticable. Freedom without virtue leads to license, and too much license leads

---

34 [Trans. note] *Neither God nor Master!* has been an anarchist motto since the 19th century. Another variation is "No god, no king, no owner, no religion, no state."

to corruption, to the collapse of character and conscience, in a word, to anarchy. It is only when an individual has gone through new and harsher trials that he or she will agree to reflect. Then the truth will come to light, and the great words of Voltaire will be realized before our eyes: "Atheism and fanaticism are the two poles of a world of confusion and horror." (In *Histoire de Jenni* [*The Story of Jenni*])

It is true that much is said about altruism or, in other words, the love of humanity. It is claimed that this sentiment should suffice. But how will one turn the love of humanity into a thing lived and realized, when one does not even arrive – I will not even say – at loving one another, but simply at giving support to one another? To group feelings and aspirations one needs a powerful ideal. Well, this ideal, you will not find it in the human being, finite and limited as it is; you will not find it in the things of this world either, all ephemeral and transient. It exists only in the infinite, eternal Being, which alone is vast enough to gather and absorb all impulsions, all forces, all aspirations of the human soul, warming and fertilizing them. This ideal is God!

But what ideal lies in it? Perfection. God being fully realized perfection is at the same time the real ideal, the living ideal!

VIII

GOD'S ACTION IN THE WORLD AND IN HISTORY

God, the core intelligence and love, is as indispensable to our inner life as the Sun is to physical life! God is the Sun of souls. It is from It that this force emanates, which is at the same time energy, thought, and light, animating and enlivening all beings. To claim that the idea of God is useless and insignificant would be the same as stating that the Sun is useless and insignificant to Nature and physical life.

Through communion of thoughts and elevation of our souls toward God, a continuous penetration occurs, like a moral fertilization of all beings, a gradual unfoldment of the powers hidden in ourselves. Such powers, namely thought and sentiment, can only be awakened and grow by means of high aspirations, by the impulsions of our hearts. If this stimulus is absent, all these latent forces remain dormant and inert in us!

I already talked about prayer. Let me explain this word again. Prayer is the most powerful form and expression of universal communion. It is not, in my view, what so many other people assume: a banal recitation, a monotonous and often repetitive exercise. By no means! True prayer, spontaneous and improvised prayer, the one that does not include formulas, makes one's soul rush toward higher regions; it draws forces and lights; it finds a support that can never be experienced or understood by those who misunderstand God and communion with It. To pray is to turn ourselves toward the eternal Being, to expose to It our thoughts and actions, to submit them to Its law and to make Its will the rule of our lives. It is to obtain by this very fact the peace of heart, the satisfaction of conscience, in a word, that inner good which is the greatest and most imperishable of all goods!

I can therefore declare that to disregard and neglect the belief in God and the communion of thought which goes with it – communion with the Soul of the universe, with this focal source from which intelligence and love forever radiate – would be the same as disregarding what is greatest in us and the universe, and despising the inner powers that make up our true wealth. It would be the same as trampling down our own happiness, everything that can produce our elevation, glory and joy.

Any individual who misunderstands God, and does not want to know what forces, what resources, and what help comes from It, nor of any communion with It, is comparable to a pauper who lives next to palaces full of treasures, risking to die of misery right in front of doors to riches open wide and inviting everyone to enter.

Sometimes we hear some skeptics say, "I don't need God!" A sad and deplorable opinion, a proud statement of those who, without God, would be nothing, would never have even existed. O blindness of the human spirit, a hundred times worse than that of the physical body! Have you ever heard a flower say, "I don't need sunshine"? Or a child say, "I don't need any parents"? Or a blind person utter, "I don't need any light"?

Then, as we know it, God is not only the light of souls; It is also love! And love is the force of all forces. Love triumphs over all brutal powers. Let us remember that if the Christian idea has conquered the ancient world, if it triumphed over the Roman power, the strength of whole armies, and the sword of the Caesars, it is because of love!

It conquered with these words: "Blessed are the meek, for they shall inherit the earth." (Matthew 5:5)

And, indeed, there is no individual, harden or cruel as he or she may be, that is not totally disarmed against you if this individual is convinced that you want their good and happiness, and is confident that your wish is genuine and selfless.

Love is all-powerful; it is the heat that melts the ice of skepticism, hatred and rage; the heat that enlivens souls that went numb, but are still capable of blooming and expanding again under this ray of love.

Note that subtle and invisible forces are indeed the true lords of the world and masters of Nature. Take electricity, for example. It weighs nothing and appears to be worthless, yet it is a marvelous force; it volatilizes metals and breaks down all bodies. The same happens with magnetism, which can paralyze the arm of a giant. Similarly, love can dominate and reduce strength; it can transform the human soul, the principle of life in ourselves, the seat of the forces of thought. That is why God, being the core universal love, is also the supreme power.

If we understand what heights, what great and noble tasks our spirits can reach through a deep understanding of the divine work and through a penetration of the thought of God into us, we would be transported with amazement and admiration.

There are those who believe that by continuing our spiritual ascension, we will eventually cease to exist, by going to destroy ourselves in the Supreme Being. This concept is serious mistaken, for, on the contrary, as reason has indicated, and as confirmed by all Higher-order Spirits, the more highly we develop intelligence and morality, the more our personality asserts itself. Every being can expand and radiate; it can grow in perception, sensation, wisdom, and love, without ever ceasing to be itself.

Do we not see it everyday in higher-order spirits which have powerful personalities? And in ourselves, do we not feel that the more we love, the more likely we are to love; that the better we understand, the more we feel able to feel and understand?

To be united to God is to feel, to realize the thought of God. But this power of feeling, this possibility of action of the spirit does not destroy the self. They can only amplify it. And when one has reached certain degrees of ascension, the soul in turn becomes one of the powers, one of the active forces of the universe; it becomes one of God's agents in the eternal work, for one's collaboration constantly expands. Its role is to transmit the divine wishes to the beings who are below it, to attract to it in its light, in its love, all that agitate, struggle and suffer in the lower worlds. It does not even content itself with hidden actions. Sometimes it incarnates taking a physical body, and becomes one of those missionaries who pass like meteors in the night of the centuries.

Then there are other theories which consist in believing that when, following its wanderings, the soul has reached absolute perfection, reaching God after a long stay in the midst of celestial beatitudes, it descends back into the material abyss, in the world of forms, at the lowest level of the scale of beings, to restart all over again the slow, tortuous and painful ascension it has just accomplished.

Theories that are not more acceptable than the other; to accept them would require a complete rejection of the notion of infinity. A notion which is necessary, although it escapes our analysis. Not much thought is necessary to be able to understand that the soul can continue its ascending march, coming closer and closer to the apogee, without ever reaching it. God is the infinite! The absolute! And despite our progress, we will never be able to compare ourselves to It, as the finite, relative, and limited beings that we are.

Every being can therefore evolve and grow incessantly, without ever achieving absolute perfection. It seems difficult to understand, and yet what can be simpler than that? Let us pick an example within the reach of everyone, a mathematical example. You take one unit – and a unity is a bit like a being – then you add to it the largest fraction you can find. This way you will get closer and closer to the number two, without ever reaching it.

We, humans, locked in the flesh, have difficulty in making an idea of the role of the spirit, which carries in it all powers, all forces of the universe; all beauties, all splendors of heavenly life; and makes them shine on the world. Nonetheless what we can and must understand is that these powerful spirits that were mentioned above, these missionaries, these agents of God, were once exactly like ourselves, humans of flesh, full of weaknesses and miseries. If they have reached so high, it was through their researches and studies, by applying God's law to all their actions and deeds. However, what they did, each of us can also do. Within ourselves, all of us have the seeds of a power and a magnitude equal to their power and their grandeur. All of us, without exception, have the same glorious destinies, the same magnificent future, and it is solely up to us to accomplish it through our innumerable lifetimes.

Thanks to psychical studies and telepathic phenomena, we are at least able to understand from now on that our faculties are not limited to our physical senses. Our spirit is capable of radiating beyond our body; it can receive influences from higher worlds, impressions of God's thought. The calls of human thought are understood by God's thought; the soul, rising above the misfortunes of the flesh, can rush toward the spiritual world which is its bequest, its future domain. This is why everyone must become their own psychical medium and learn how to communicate with the higher world of the spirits.

Up to now, this power had been the privilege of a few initiates. Today it is necessary for everyone to acquire it, and for every human to grasp and understand the manifestations of higher thought. We can achieve it through a pure and unblemished life, and by gradually training our psychical faculties.

God's action is revealed in the universe, both in the physical and in the moral world; not a single being is left out of Its solicitude. We see It manifest itself in the majestic law of progress which presides over the evolution of beings and things, bringing them to an ever more perfect state. This action is also shown in the history of civilizations. Through the eras, we can follow through this great march, this push of humanity toward Good, toward Better. No doubt, throughout this centuries-old march, there have been many failures and setbacks, many sad and somber hours, but we must always bear in mind that humans are free to choose their actions. Their ills are almost always the consequence of their errors while in an inferior state of evolution.

Is it not by providential choice that certain individuals seem destined to bring into this world great innovations, major discoveries that contribute to the advancement of civilizations? Such discoveries are all linked together, appearing one after the other, in methodical and regular order, as they can successfully be grafted onto progress previously achieved.

What demonstrates in a striking way the intervention of God in history, is the appearance at appointed times, at solemn hours, of these great missionaries, who come to reach out to everyone in order to put them back on the right path which they lost, by teaching them the moral law, loving fellowship, the love of neighbor, while also giving them the great example of self-sacrifice on behalf of humankind.

Is there anything more imposing than this role of the divine envoys? They come, they walk among the nations. In vain sarcasms and taunts rain upon them. In vain contempt and suffering await them at every step. They always walk on! In vain gallows and scaffolds are raised around them. Bonfires are lit: They go ahead, their foreheads high, their souls serene. What is the secret of their strength? Who or what drives them forward?

Above the shadows of matter and the coarseness of life, higher than Earth, higher than humanity, they see the eternal core shine forth, whose ray illuminates them and gives them the courage to confront all horrors, all tortures and pain. They have contemplated the truth without veils, and henceforth they have no other concern than to spread, to put within the reach of crowds, the knowledge of the great laws which govern both souls and worlds!

All these powerful spirits declared to come in the name of God in order to execute his will. Jesus often said, "It was my father who sent me." And Joan of Arc was no less precise when she said, "I come from God, to deliver France from the English."

All these powerful spirits declared to come in the name of God in order to execute his will. Jesus often said, "It was my father who sent me." And Joan of Arc is no less precise: "I come from God, to deliver France from the English."

In the midst of the frightful night represented by the 15th century, in that abyss of miseries and sorrows in which the life and honor of a great nation had fallen, what did Joan of Arc bring to France, then betrayed, conquered, and dying? Was it material help, soldiers, an army? No, what she brought was faith, faith in oneself, faith in the future of France, faith in God! "I come from the King of Heaven," she said, "and bring you the help of heaven." And with this faith, France has recovered, escaping destruction and death!

The same occurs today! There is only one remedy, either to sarcastic skepticism, or to discouragement and despair, which invade us from all sides.

There is only one remedy for this depression of thought and conscience, for this disgust of life, which is found for example in so many suicides. This remedy is faith in ourselves, in our immortal destinies; faith in that supreme Power which never abandons those who have placed their trust in it.

The only means of saving society when it is in peril, lest it sink into anarchy, is to raise our thoughts and hearts, all the aspirations of the human soul, toward that infinite Power which is God; it is to unite our will with Its will, and to let us be impregnated by its law – this is the secret of all strength, of all elevation!

And we shall be surprised and marveled, as we go down this forgotten path, at acknowledging and discovering that God is not a metaphysical abstraction, an ideal concept lost in the depths of a dream, or as the saying goes, an ideal that does not exist, as preached by Vacherot and Renan, among other materialists! No, they were wrong, God is a living, sentient, and conscious Being; God is an active reality. God is our parent, our guide, our comforter, our very best friend. As long as we direct our appeals to God and open our hearts to It, God will enlighten us with Its light, warm us with Its love. It will pour upon us Its immense Soul, a Soul rich in all perfections. By God and through God alone we will truly feel as loving fellow beings, living in happiness. Away from God we can only find darkness, uncertainty, disappointment, pain and moral misery! This is the assistance that Joan of Arc brought to France, as is the assistance now brought by Modern Spiritualism (i.e., Spiritism) to all humanity!

We can therefore affirm that the God's thought has shined throughout history and over the whole world: it has inspired countless generations in their march, sustaining them, and relieving millions from their sorrows. It has been the strength, the supreme hope, the last support of the afflicted, the despoiled, the sacrificed, and of almost everyone who has suffered through the ages from injustice and wickedness of fellow humans, or felt the blows of adversity!

If you evoke the memory of generations which have succeeded one another on Earth, you will see the eyes of the human race everywhere turning toward this light that nothing can extinguish or diminish!

Therefore I say to you, my fellow human beings: Gather in the silence of your dwellings; frequently raise up to God the impulsions of your thoughts and hearts; expose to It all your needs, your weaknesses, your miseries; and, when facing hard times, at solemn moments of your lives, address to It the supreme appeal. Then, in the most intimate part of your being, you will hear something similar to a voice answer you, soothe and assist you. This voice will penetrate you with deep emotion; it may bring forth tears, but in the end you will be strengthened and comforted it.

Learn to pray from the depths of your soul, instead of your lips and the tips of your tongues; learn to enter into communion with the Creator, and to receive these mysterious teachings not reserved to scholars or to the powerful, but to pure souls and sincere hearts.

When you wish to find refuge from the sadness and disappointments of the world, remember that there is only one way: to raise one's thoughts toward those pure regions of divine light, where coarse earthly influences cannot penetrate. The rumors of passions, the conflict of interests are not able to reach that far. Once arriving at these regions, the spirit emerges from its inferior concerns, from all the petty things of human existence. It hovers above the human tempest, higher than the jarring sounds of life struggles, of our fight for wealth and vain honors; higher than all those ephemeral and changing things which bind us to the material world. Up there the spirit lights up, intoxicated with the splendors of truth and light. Then it can see and understand the laws that govern its destiny.

Faced with the broad perspectives of immortality, before the spectacle of the progress and the ascension that await us on the ladder of worlds, what importance do our current vicissitudes have, these miseries of present life?

Those who have in their thoughts and in their hearts such an ardent faith, such an absolute confidence in the future, such certainty that elevates them, are armored against pain. They will remain invulnerable in the midst of trials. This is the secret of all strength, of all valor, the secret of the innovators, the martyrs, of all those who, through the centuries, have given their lives for a great cause; of all those who, amidst tortures, under the executioner's hand, while their bones and flesh were crushed by the wheel and the easel, and reduced to a bloody pulp, still managed to find strength to dominate their sufferings and affirm God's justice. Those who, on the scaffold as well as on the stake, already lived by anticipation the glorious and imperishable life of the spirit!

IX

OBJECTIONS AND CONTRADICTIONS

As it is the largest, deepest problem, encompassing all the others, the divine problem has given rise to theories, countless systems, which correspond to so many degrees of human comprehension, to so many different stages of thought, as it moves toward the Absolute.

In this field, contradictions abound. Every religion explains God in its own way; each theory describes It in its own manner. And all this results in confusion, an inextricable chaos. What varied forms of the idea of God, from the fetish of the Africans to the Parabrahm of the Hindus, to the Pure Act of St. Thomas Aquinas! From this confusion, atheists have drawn arguments to deny the existence of God; positivists declare God to be "unknowable."

How to remedy such a disorder? How to escape these contradictions? It is very simple indeed: It is enough to rise above all theories and systems, high enough to connect them as a whole, by what they have in common. It suffices to rise to the grand Cause, in which everything is summed up and explained.

A narrowness of views has distorted and compromised the idea of God. Remove the barriers, the shackles, the closed systems that contradict each other, excluding one another, fighting each other, and instead substitute them with broad views of higher conceptions. At certain heights, science, philosophy, religion, all hitherto divided, opposed, and hostile in their inferior forms, unite and merge into a powerful synthesis which is that of Modern Spiritualism.

This is how the law of evolution of ideas is fulfilled. After the thesis, we have the antithesis. Now we touch on the synthesis, which will sum up all forms and beliefs, thus becoming the glory of the 20th century to have it established and formulated.

Let us take a quick look at the most frequent objections. The most common one is that which consists in saying: if God exists, if It is, as purported, Goodness, Justice, and Love, why do evil and suffering reign supreme around us? So God is good, yet millions of poor people suffer in their souls and in their flesh. All is pain and tears in the lives of crowds. Iniquity is sovereign all over our globe, and the feverish struggle for survival makes countless victims every day.

As I have shown elsewhere,[35] suffering is a powerful means of education for all souls. It develops sensitivity, which is already in itself an increase in life. Sometimes it is one of the forms of justice, a corrective to our previous or distant deeds.

Evil is only the consequence of human imperfection. If God had created perfect beings, evil would not exist. But then, the universe would be frozen, immobile in its monotonous perfection. The magnificent ascension of souls through infinity would be suppressed. Nothing to conquer; nothing else to desire! Now, what would be of perfection without merits, without efforts to obtain it? Would it be of any value in our eyes?

In short, evil is but the least evolving toward the most, the inferior toward the superior, the soul toward God.

---

35 See Léon DENIS, *After Death* (Trans. G. G. Fleurot, J. Korngold. New York: USSF, 2017), second part; *The Problem of Life & Destiny* (Trans. H. M. Monteiro. New York: USSF, 2018), ch. XVIII–XIX.

God made us free; hence the evil, a transitional phase in our ascension. Freedom is a necessary condition for diversity in universal unity. Without it, monotony would have made the universe unbearable. God has given us freedom with this initial impulse of life whereby the being will evolve through its own effort, over boundless space and time, on the ladder of successive lives, on the surface of the worlds that populate the cosmos.

We emanate from God same as our thoughts emanate from our mind, without splitting it, without diminishing it in any way. Once free and accountable, we become masters and artisans of our own destinies. But in order to develop the latent potentials and forces which exist within us, struggle is necessary – a struggle against matter, against human passions, against all that we call evil. This struggle is painful and contains many failures. Yet, little by little, experience is acquired, our will is tempered, good emerges from evil. A time comes when the soul triumphs over inferior influences, redeems itself, and elevates itself through expiation and purification even to a joyful living. Then it understands, it comes to admire the wisdom and foresight of God, which, by making it the arbiter of its own destiny, has arranged all things so as to release the greatest amount of happiness for each and everyone of us.

The present condition of every soul is the just outcome of its past lives. In the same way, our present existence gives birth, day by day, though our free will, to the fate that we will face in future.

Other objections arise. There is one that we cannot ignore because it is one of the most important questions in philosophy. The question proposed is as follows: Is God a personal being, or is It the universal, infinite Being? It cannot be both, because, so they say, these conceptions are different and mutually exclusive. Hence, the two great systems on God: deism[36] and pantheism. In reality, this contradiction is only due to a distortion of views from the human spirit, which cannot understand either the personality or the infinite.

The true personality is the self, one's intelligence, one's will, one's conscience. Nothing prevents us from conceiving it as limitless, that is, infinite. God, being perfection itself, cannot be limited. Thus two apparently contradictory notions are reconciled.

There is still another point: Is God the unknowable, as positivists claim, together with Berthelot? Is God the abyss of the Gnostics, the veiled Isis of the temples of Egypt, the redoubtable and mysterious Holy of Holies of the Hebrews – or can God be known?

The answer could not be easier: God is unknowable in Its essence, in Its intimate depths, but It reveals itself through all its work, in this great book open before our eyes and in the depths of ourselves.

Elsewhere, it is still emphasized: You have told us that the essential purpose of life, of all our lives, is to enter more and more into universal communion, to better love and better serve God in Its purposes. Since God cannot be known in its fullness, how could one love and serve the unknown?

Undoubtedly, no one can know God in Its essence – I would say – but we know It by its admirable laws, by the plan which It traced for all existences, and in which Its wisdom and justice are eminently in evidence. To love God, it is not necessary to separate It from its work, God

---

36 [Transl. note] Compare *deism* with *theism*.

must be seen in its universality, in the flow of life and love that It pours upon all things. God is not the unknown, It is only the unseen.

The soul, our thoughts, good, moral beauty are also invisible. And yet, should we not love them? And to love them, is it not yet to love God which is their source, since It is at once the supreme thought, the perfect beauty, and the absolute good!

In essence, we do not understand any of these principles. Yet we know that they exist and we cannot escape their influence and exempt ourselves from worshiping them. If we only loved what we know and understand in fullness, what would we love, limited as we are right now, in the narrow bounds of our earthly understanding!

To those who absolutely require a definition, I could then say that God is pure spirit, pure idea and thought. But a pure idea, in its essence, cannot be formulated without being immediately diminished and altered as a result. Every formula is a prison. Enclosed in the jail of words, thought loses its radiance, its brilliance, when it does not lose its true and extended meaning. Impoverished and deformed, it becomes subject to criticism and thus sees what is most convincing in itself vanish.

On the spiritual plane, thought is a brilliant image. Compared to thought expressed by human words, it is like a young child resplendent with life and beauty, as compared to the same young child lying in a coffin, in the rigid and frozen forms of death.

Nonetheless, in spite of our inability to express it in all its extent, the idea of God is essential, as I have said, since it is indispensable to our life. We have just seen that the essence of Good, Truth, and Beauty escape our grasp because they are all of divine nature. Our own intelligence, in its turn, is incomprehensible to us precisely because it contains a divine particle which endows it with lofty faculties. And it is only by penetrating the mystery of the human soul that, one day, we all will be able to solve the enigma of the infinite Being.

God is in us as we are in It. God is the great focal point of life and love, of which every soul is a spark, or rather a small focal point, still obscure and veiled, which contains all powers in embryonic state. So much so that if we knew all that lies within us and the magnificent deeds we can achieve, we would transform the world; we would jump-start it, taking a leap onto the immense path of progress.

To know ourselves, we must therefore study God, for all that is in God is in us, at least in embryonic state. God is the universal spirit that expresses itself and manifests itself in Nature, and the human being is the highest expression of Nature.

All human beings must arrive at this understanding of their superior nature; for it is the ignorance of this nature and the resources that remain asleep in us that cause of all our trials, failures and falls.

That is why we will say to all: let us rise above quarrels among different schools of thought, above vain discussions and polemics. Let us rise high enough to understand that we are something other than a cog in the blind machine of the world: we are children of God and, as such, closely bound to It and its work; destined for an immense purpose, next to which everything else becomes secondary. Our ultimate goal is the entrance into the holy harmony of beings and things, which can only be realized in God and by God!

Let us rise up to that lofty point, and we will feel the power that lies within ourselves; we will understand the role that we are called to play in the work of eternal progress. Let us not forget that we are immortal spirits. Earthly things are but a stepping stone for us, a means of education, of transformation. We can lose all material goods while on Earth. What does it really matter? What we need above all is to enlarge, to tear from its coarse maze, that divine spirit, that inner god which is in every individual the source of their greatness, of their future happiness. This is the ultimate goal of life!

Summing up: God is the great soul of the universe, the focal point from which emanate all life, all moral light. You cannot do without God any more than the Earth and all beings living on its surface cannot do without the solar source. Would the Sun suddenly go out, what would happen? Our planet would roll in the emptiness of the cosmos, carrying away with it its humanity forever perished in a sepulcher of ice. All things would be dead, the globe would turn into a huge necropolis. A gloomy silence would reign over the great cities now forever asleep.

So there! God is the sun of souls! Turn off the idea of God and immediately a moral night will fall over the world. It is precisely because the idea of God is falsified, distorted by some; repulsed, misunderstood by many others; that currently humanity wanders in the midst of storms, without a crew, without compass, without guidance, and prey to disorder, abandoned to all sorts of sorrow.

To elevate, to enlarge the idea of God, to rid it of the dross with which religions and systems have enveloped it, this is the role of Modern Spiritualism (i.e. Spiritism)!

If so many individuals are still unable to see and understand the supreme harmony of laws, beings, and things, it is because their souls have not yet entered their inner sense of communication with God; in other words, those divine thoughts that illuminate the universe and are the imperishable light of the world.

In conclusion, I hope that I have succeeded in giving a glimpse of the idea of God. The human word is very limited, very dry and cold to deal with such a subject. Only harmony itself, the great symphony of the spheres, the voice of the infinite, could render and express the universal law. There are things so profound that they should be felt and not described. God alone, in its boundless love, can reveal to us its hidden meaning. And that is what It will do, if in our faith, in our constant impetus toward truth, we learn how to present to the One which probes the most mysterious folds of our consciousness, a soul capable of understanding It, a heart worthy of loving It!

PART TWO

THE BOOK
OF
NATURE

X

THE STARRY SKIES

A magnificent book, as said above, opens before our eyes. In it, every patient observer can read the wording of the enigma, the secret of eternal life. We see therein a unique will has disposed the majestic order in which all destinies shake, all existences move, all spirits and hearts pulsate.

O soul! Learn first the supreme lesson that descends from the spiritual plane upon anxious brows. The Sun is hidden under the horizon; its last glimmers of light still tinge the sky; a softened light indicates that, up there, a star has been veiled from our eyes. The night spreads above our heads its dome studded with stars. Our thought collects itself and seeks the secret of things. Let us turn to the East. The Milky Way unrolls like an immense scarf its myriads of stars, looking so squashed together, and so far away that they seem to form a continuous mass. Everywhere, as the night gets darker, other stars appear, other flames light up like lamps suspended in the divine sanctuary. Through unfathomable depths, these orbs send each other their silver rays; they impress us at a distance and speak to us in a mute language.

They do not all shine with equal brilliance; therefore the powerful Sirius is not comparable to the distant Capella. Their vibrations have taken centuries to reach us, and each of their rays is like a song, a melody, a penetrating voice. These songs can be summarized as follows: *We too are focal points of life, suffering and evolution. Thousands of souls fulfill in us destinies similar to yours.*

However, not all use the same language, for some are openings for peace and bliss, while others are worlds of struggle, atonement, and repair through pain. Some seem to say: I have known you, human soul, earthly soul; I have known you and I will see you again! I sheltered you in my womb once and you will come back to me. I am waiting for you so as to guide in your turn the beings who are moving on my surface!

And then, further still, this star which seems lost in the depths of the abyss of the sky and whose trembling light is hardly perceptible; this star will say to us: I know that you will pass through the orbs which form my retinue and are flooded with my rays; I know that you will suffer there and that you will become better there. Speed up on your ascension. I will be and I am already a friend, because your thoughts have risen to me; your pleading, your questioning, your prayer to God have reached me.

Thus, all the stars sing their poem of life and love to us. They all make us hear a powerful evocation of the past or of the future. They are "the mansions of our Father," so to speak; stages, superb milestones on the roads of the infinite. And we shall pass through them, one day we will all live there in order to penetrate the eternal divine light.

Spaces and worlds! What wonders have you reserved for us? Immense seas, unfathomable depths, which all give reflect divine majesty. In you, everywhere and always, is harmony, splendor, beauty! Before you, all pride melts away, all vain glories vanish. Here, riding their immense orbs, there are stars of fire near which our Sun is but a pale torch. Each of them leads after itself an imposing train of spheres, which represent so many realms of evolution. There, as on Earth, sentient beings live, love, and suffer. Their trials and their common struggles create between them bonds of affection which then grow little by little.

And this is how souls begin to feel the first fragrance of this love that God wants to make known to all beings. Farther on, in the inscrutable abyss, marvelous worlds keep orbiting, inhabited by pure souls which once experienced suffering and sacrifice, and now have reached the summit of perfection. Souls that contemplate God in Its glory, and move, without ever getting tired, from star to star, from planetary system to planetary system, carrying the divine designs into effect. They already have in them something of this infinity which merges with eternity.

All these stars seem to smile at us like forgotten friends. Their mysteries attract us. We feel like they are our inheritance, bestowed by God. In future centuries, we will get to know all these wonders that our thoughts can barely touch. We will go through the infinite, which we cannot describe in our narrow language. Indeed, there are in this ascension so many degrees that we are not able to count them; but our spirit guides will help us climb them by teaching us how to spell the letters of gold and fire, the divine language of light and love. Then time will become measureless to us, distances will cease to exist. We will no longer think of the obscure, tortuous and steep paths followed by us in the past. Instead we will aspire to those serene joys of beings which came long before us, and which have traced, by rays of light, our everlasting path. The worlds where we lived will have vanished, becoming nothing but dust and debris, but we will keep the delightful impressions of happiness gathered on their surfaces, effusions from the heart that set forth the unity between ourselves and other sibling souls. We will also preserve the dear and painful memory of shared evils; and will no longer be separated from those we loved – for bonds between souls are like those between the stars. Throughout centuries and heavenly places, we will rise up together toward God, the great focal point of love which attracts all created beings!

XI

THE FOREST

O human soul! Go back down to Earth, collect yourself, turn the pages of its book open to all eyes; read in the layers of the soil that you tread, the story of the slow formation of worlds, the action of immense forces taking place on the globe to prepare it for the life of civilizations, nations, and societies.

Then listen carefully! Listen to the harmonies of Nature, the mysterious sounds of forests, the echoes of mountains and valleys, the hymn murmured by torrents in the silence of the night. Listen to the great voice of the sea! Everywhere resounds the song of beings and things, the rustling life, the plaint of souls who already suffer as we do, making an effort to free themselves from the material bondage that enchains them.

The forest stretches up to the distant horizon its masses of greenery which quiver in the breeze and wave from hill to hill. Through the heavy foliage, light pours itself in golden rays upon the tree trunks and into the mosses; and the wind blows playfully through the branches. Autumn adds a symphony of colors to all these delights, from yellowish green to tawny red and pure golden hues. It shines and scorches the thickets, tinting with ocher the chestnut trees, with purple the beech trees, and making the pink mantles of heath glow on the glades.

Let us get into the dense foliage. As we advance, the forest envelops us in its fragrance and mystery. Fertile scents rise from the ground; plants exhale a subtle aroma. A powerful magnetism emerges from the giant trees, penetrating and intoxicating us. Therein, golden beams descend upon the trunks of the birches, making them shine like the colonnades of a temple. Farther on, dark trees rise up, cut in a straight line by an alley which extends, as far as the eye can see, its arches of greenery, like vaults of a cathedral. On all sides, retreats full of shadow and silence open deep niches of solitude that inspire a beguiling emotion in us. You walk there in thick darkness riddled by rays of sunshine.

Here, a venerable beech tree rounds its leafy domes to the sides of a hill. There, oaks lean their thick foliage over a pond's mirror. A centuries-old tree, elder of the woods, spared by the ax – and so big that three or four humans could not embrace it – stands isolated, high as a church. Tempest lightning may often visit it, managing to break a few of its branches, but this tree remains standing regardless, always proud and protective. On its foot, felted with moss and swollen with monstrous roots, we find beetles running over its rough bark like precious stones.

In melancholy solitude, pines show their reddish boles and twisted branches in the shape of a lyre. Could it be a whim of Nature? After all, the pine is the musical tree par excellence. Its fine and flexible needles sway in the wind in plaintive melodies; its singing branches are full of caresses and whisperings.

How nice it is to wander under the silent and shivering shade of the great woods, along the clear brook and the vague footprints left by the deers! How sweet it is to lie down on the velvet mosses or the carpets made of fern, at the bottom of some granitic rock. To follow with your eyes the race of golden beetles in the grass, or the small lizards on the stones, and lend the ear to the happy twittering of birds! An unseen world moves and rustles around us: a concert of the infinitely small, cradling the Earth to rest. Insects, by myriads, conduct their rounds in a ray of light, while at the top of an aspen, a warbler sings its lungs out in pearly roulades. Here, everything is joy of living and a fertile metamorphosis!

Amidst a bunch of trees, a spring spouts from the rocks; it spread itself on a bed of pebbles, all through bindweed and bellflowers, wild mints and sage. From the basin carved by its waters, where the titmice come to drink, the crystalline wave drips drop by drop, then runs softly. The shadow cast by a large pine shelters and protects a cute conch shell. The wind waves the pine's needles, while the spring murmurs its melody. A ray of the Sun, sliding through the branches, comes and adds a thousand sparkling reflections to the limpid surface of the water. In the air, dragonflies dance and frolic; pretty multicolored flies buzz in the chalices of variegated flowers.

In the peaceful landscape, the noise of running, babbling water is a symbol of human life, which emerges from the dark depths of the past and then flees, without ever stopping, to the oceans of destiny, where God leads it through ever higher, ever fresher and new tasks. A small spring, a little stream, these friends of philosophers and thinkers, talk to me of the other side, to which I move every single second, and remind me that everything around us is a lesson, teaching all those who are able to see, listen, and understand, the language of beings and things!

But, suddenly, the howling southerly wind rises; a powerful breath passes over the forest, vibrating like an immense pipe organ. Similar to a tide of emerald, the great flow of vegetation swells little by little, a great bustle and noise ensue. An invisible choir animates the fierce wilderness. The gigantic tree trunks writhe with long moans. Clangors rise from the thickets, like chariot bearings or clashing armies.

The path climbs to a plateau and meanders through a chestnut wood. These ancient trees tremble in the wind. By inclining their heavily loaded branches, they seem to say to us humans: Come and pick my fruit, in which we have distilled the sap of our marrows; take my dead branches, which in winter will warm your homes. Take it all, but be neither ungrateful nor indifferent, for all Nature works for you. So do not be ungrateful, otherwise the hardships, the harsh lessons of adversity will inevitably soften your heart, and tear you away sooner or later from your insouciance, your doubts, your errors; and eventually direct your thinking toward an understanding of the Great Law!

Soon the force of the landscape changes and eases up. The wind softens. The moor takes over from the forest; gorse, lavender, and broom follow the imposing assembly of the woods. On a bulge in the ground surface, a tall monolith stands at the center of a circle of mossy stones, some still standing, others lying in the grass, telling the story of ancient civilizations, with their dreams, traditions, and beliefs.[37] The spectacle offered by these enigmatic stones plunges me back into the depths of time. A melancholy of vanished things emerges from it, while around us nature gives us the sensation of eternal youth.

Valleys open, ravines deepen along the slopes. Under the foliage and fragrant bushes, fountains rise up pure and fresh, filling the valley with their murmurs. Now the day is declining. Through the gorges, in a bluish indentation, the Sun casts reflections of purple and gold. Fiery hues glow on the edge of the woods. Behind me, gilt by the glittering setting Sun, the great forest spreads its giant trees and dense bushes, all forming the sumptuous and charming mantle with which autumn has adorned it. The oblique rays of

---

[37] [Trans. note] Here Léon DENIS is referring especially to the Gauls and Celts of ancient Europe.

the Sun glide through the colonnades and illuminate distant solitudes, highlighting the multicolored foliage with various browns, tawny ores, brilliant reds, chromes and lacquered tones. Everything is lit up, everything blazes in a sort of apotheosis in this magical scenery, which dazzles me in its peaceful sunset, exalting my thought and making it ascend and soar toward the Cause of so many wonders, to glorify It!

~~~

Everything in the forest is enchanting, whether in spring, when the powerful sap swells its thousand arteries and young shoots and buds come with green galore; or when autumn adorns it with fiery hues and glamorous colors; or even when winter turns it into a magical palace made of crystal, whether bent under the snow by darkened tree branches, or transformed into Christmas trees hung with many diamond pendants.

Yet the forest is not just a wondrous sight; it is also a perpetual lesson. It constantly teaches us strong rules, the solemn principles that govern all life and preside over the renewal of beings and seasons. To the turbulent and restless, it offers its retreats, which are deep and conducive to reflection. To the impatient and those eager to enjoy, it tells that nothing is durable that has not taken the trouble and time to sprout, to emerge from the shadows and climb to the skies. To the violent and impulsive, it opposes the view of its slow evolution. It brings calm to febrile souls. Sympathetic to joys, compassionate to human sorrows, it dresses bruised hearts. It comforts, gives rest, and imparts to all obscure forces, energies hidden in its bosom. The legend of Antaeus[38] is always applicable to the wounds of existence, to all those who have exhausted their personal abilities and vital powers in the bitter struggles of life in this world. It suffices for them to reconnect with Nature in order to regain unlimited resources in the secret virtue that emerges thereof.

And how many analogies and lessons we can find in all these things! The acorn, under its modest envelope, contains not only a whole oak in its majestic blossoming, but also a whole forest. Tinier still, a seed holds in its tidy cradle, the whole flower with all its grace, colors, and perfume. In the same way, the human soul has in latent state all the development of its faculties, of its powers to come. If we could watch the spectacle of vegetable metamorphoses, we would find it hard to believe. Likewise, the evolutionary cycle of souls in their infinite ascension escape us, and currently we cannot comprehend all the splendor of their becoming. Yet we have an example of this in all great geniuses of humanity, who have passed through history as dazzling comets, leaving behind imperishable works. Such are the heights to which even the most backward souls on the ladder of innumerable lives can eventually rise, with the aid of two essential factors: time and work!

Thus Nature has shown in everything the beauty of life, the reward of patient and courageous effort, and is giving us an image of our own endless destinies. It tells us that each and everything has its place in the universe, whether souls or things; and also, that they must all evolve and transforms themselves. Death is only apparent: gloomy winters are followed by the revival of spring, full of promise and

---

38 [Trans. note] According to Greek mythology, *Antaeus* compelled all strangers who were passing through the country to wrestle with him. Whenever Antaeus touched the earth (his mother), his strength was renewed (*Encyclopædia Britannica*, 9th ed., vol. II, Edinburgh: Adam & Charles Black, 1875).

life-giving sap. The law which governs our existence is not different from that of the seasons. After the sunny days of summer, winter comes like old age, and with it the hope of rebirth and a new youth. Nature, like us, loves and suffers. Everywhere, under the flow of love that overwhelms the universe, we find a current of pain. However, it is salutary since, by refining the sensitivity of living beings, it awakens in them the latent qualities of emotion and tenderness, thus adding up to their lives.

The forest is the ornament of the earth and the true preserver of the world. Without it, the soil, carried away by the rains, would soon return to the depths of the immense sea. The forest holds the large drops of the storm in its moss mats, and in the entanglement of its roots. It saves them for the springs and releases them little by little, transformed, turned into fertilizing, no longer devastating agents. Wherever trees disappear, the soil becomes poorer, losing its beauty. Gradually monotony is followed by aridity, then death ensues. A revitalizer par excellence, the breathing of its billions of leaves[39] distill the air and purify the atmosphere.

As we have seen, the role of the forest is no less considerable from a psychical viewpoint. The forest has always been the refuge of collected and dreamy thought. How many delicate and powerful works have been conceived in its fresh and moving shadows, in the peace of its imposing and cozy branches! Whoever possesses the soul of an artist,

---

[39] One birch alone, says the geographer Onésime RECLUS, has two hundred thousand leaves, while a giant one from the tropics, may carry a million.

a writer, or a poet, will be able to draw from this living source plenty of fruitful inspirations.

With its majestic rhythm, the forest cradled the childhood of religions. Sacred architecture, in its most audacious boldness, has only copied it. Are the Gothic naves of our cathedrals anything but an imitation in stone of the thousand colonnades and the imposing vaults of the woods? The voice of the pipe organs, is it not the shuddering of the wind which, at varying hours of day and night, sighs through the pipe reeds or makes the tall pines groan? The forest has served as a model for the highest manifestations of the religious idea in its esthetic development. In the early ages it covered almost the entire surface of the planet. Nothing was more impressive to our ancestors than the ancient deep sylva of Gaul, with its mysterious grandeur and natural sanctuaries, where the sacred rites used to be performed – its retreats sometimes full of horror, when the rumblings of the storm were echoed by the woods, and the cry of wild beasts rose from the bosom of the thickets; full of charm and poetry. And where, once calmness was restored and the blue sky and the bright light reappeared through the branches, birds sang in celebration of life's eternal feast.

From century to century, the Celtic soul has kept the strong imprint of the primitive forest and a love for its sanctuaries, sojourns of tutelary spirits that Vercingetorix[40] and Joan of Arc honored, listening to their inspiring voices in the green solitude.

The Celtic mindset is eager for clarity and space and always passionate for freedom. It possesses a profound intuition of the things of the soul which claim direct revelation, a personal communion with the visible and invisible

---

40 [Trans, note] Vercingetorix (? – 46 BC), "Chieftain of the Gallic tribe of the Arverni whose formidable rebellion against Roman rule was crushed by Julius Caesar" (*Encyclopædia Britannica*).

Nature. That is why it will always remain in opposition to the Roman Church, which is defiant of Nature, and whose doctrine is all about oppression and authority. The druids and the bards were rebellious. In spite of the Roman conquest and barbarian invasions which facilitated the expansion of Christianity, the Celtic soul, by a sort of instinct, always felt to be the inheritor of a wider and freer faith than that of Rome.

In vain would Catholic monks seek to impose on it the idea of asceticism and renunciation, submission to rigid dogmas, and to a lugubrious conception of death and the hereafter. The Celtic spirit, in its ardent thirst for knowledge, for living and acting, would always escape this narrow circle.

The fundamental idea of Celtic Druidism was evolution, the idea of progress and development with freedom. This idea was borrowed, to a certain extent, from nature and supplemented by revelation. In fact, the general impression that emerged from the spectacle of the world was a feeling of harmony, a notion of being linked, an idea of purpose and law, that is to say, of the eternal relationships of beings and things. The evolutionary conception emerges from the study of these laws. There was a direction, a finality in evolution, and this direction carried the whole of life, by imperceptible gradations taking centuries to come to completion, toward an ever-better state.

Christianity, or rather Catholicism, has dismissed this idea, but new scientific discoveries brings us back to it. First, it spiritualizes matter by reducing it to centers of forces. It shows us the nervous system becoming more and more complex in the scale of beings until it reaches human species. Wild species tend to disappear in the face of human superiority. With the development of the brain, thought triumphs. The consciousness accomplishes its parallel ascension. There is a reconciliation between moral laws and physical and biological certainties. The order which manifests itself in both domains leads to analogous conclusions: Nature is as plastic as consciousness, and equally mobile, being influenced by the divine Spirit.

As evolution is the central law of the universe, the main role of social order is to facilitate it to all its members. Life is good, useful and fruitful. Next to the infinite perspectives which it opens to us, all the depressing feelings, such as, pessimism, doubt, sadness and despair, vanish to make room for immortal aspirations, and imperishable hope.

This was the genius of the Celtic civilization, lingering on the flood of invasions, surviving all the vicissitudes of history, reappearing in many different guises, after periods of eclipse and silence, which explains the great mission and influence of France in the work of civilization. More than any other people, the Celts, whose origins are lost in extremely ancient mists of time, approach, by some sort of hereditary instinct, the world of causes and sources of life. Both in science and in philosophy, many times they have succeeded in bringing astray thought back to the focused feeling of Nature and its revealing laws, to a clearer conception of the eternal principles. If Celtic enthusiasm and faith could be extinguished, there would be less light and joy in the world, less passionate impulses towards truth and goodness. For over a century, German materialism has darkened thought, paralyzing its growth. We can observe everywhere, around us, the fatal results of its influence. But here is the Celtic genius reappearing in the form of Modern Spiritualism (i.e., Spiritism), to enlighten again the human soul in its ascension: it offers to all those whose lips are parched by the harsh wind of life, a cup of hope and immortality from which to drink.[41]

---

41 [Trans. note] Current readers should bear in mind that Léon DENIS was a Frenchman whose exalted patriotism included even the Celts. His obvious bias against the Germans came from World War I.

XII

THE SEA

O n the deck of the ship that carries me away, I gaze at the immensity of the sea waters. Until the ends of the firmament, the sea spreads its deep expanse, moving and sparkling in the daylight. Not a single cloud; not the slightest noise. The Sun of the south lights up the crest of the waves, glinted with fugitive gleams. On this vast mirror, the sunlight is played in delicate nuances and swiftly changing ripples. It envelops islands, promontories and beaches with a light clarity; it softens the horizon, idealizing the distant perspectives. A few passengers aboard the ship take a nap, the deck is deserted. The silence is disturbed only by the sound of the propeller and the murmur of the wave, which gently caresses the flanks of the ship. Everywhere around us deep peace reigns. Nowhere have I had such a relaxing impression. It is like an appeasement, a serenity, a detachment from everything, forgetting the miseries of human agitations, and producing a dilation of the soul, a kind of voluptuousness of life and certainty that life will last forever; in short, the sensation that we are as imperishable as this infinity of earth and sky.

The golden shores of Provence (France) seem to flee aways, as the bow of the liner, now facing Africa, splits the blue waters. The Mediterranean is utterly enchanting under an azure sky; but all the seas have their own prestige, their beauty, whether in days of inclement weather, with the moving fascination of their foaming waves; or at the periods of calm, with the splendor of their sunsets. Their boundless horizons lead the soul to a state of contemplation of eternal things and divine dreams. Almost all sailors are idealists and believers.

〜

The shores of France are washed by two different seas. The Mediterranean is beautiful for the harmony of its outlines, the limpidity of its atmosphere, the richness of its colors.

The Atlantic Ocean is as imposing in its periods of turbulence as it is in its periods of calm, with its large waves breaking against the coast twice a day; under an agitated sky, often clouded, and its great purifying breath. It is especially from the promontories of the Armorica[42] princes, that the ocean is majestic to behold in its hours of wrath, when the waves rush upon the reefs, roaring in the deep and secret coves, or rolling with thunder in the shadow of the caverns dug in the rock. The moan of the sea sounds somewhat penetrating and solemn, which makes the solitudes sadder and more impressive. The calls of the curlews, seagulls, and other maritime birds which fly in a whirling motion in the midst of the storm, add to the desolation of the scene. The whole coast is white with foam. Under the feet of the observer, the ground trembles at every surge of the breakers.

From the Cape of the Goat, Raz de Sein, and the Point of Penmarch (all in France), the scenery is equally epic and wildly magnificent. Everywhere masses of blackened rocks extend the continent like a multitude of fragments torn from the skeleton of the globe by the fury of the waters. Long lines of debris lengthen, testifying to the

---

[42] [Transl. note] *Armorican*, from Armorica (Brittany), part of ancient Gaul.

centuries-old struggles that the incessant flow delivers to the harsh granite. All in all, a formidable chaos, where the unleashed elements swirl and rush on the earth, moaning under their redoubled efforts.

Now the sea has calmed down, so has the wind. Evening has fallen, and bright stars scintillate in the deep blue sky. Lighthouse beacons shine and blink on, as they light up the roads off the coast. Silence is made, disturbed only by the imposing monotonous chant of the ocean, which rises, slowly, grave, and continuous, like a psalmody or incantation. What is it telling us? Like all the harmonies of Nature, it speaks of the supreme Cause of everything, of the God's immense work. It reminds us how small we humans really are in our material form, next to the majesty of the waters and the sky; yet how great we can be for having a soul that can embrace all things, savor all beauties, and reveal all teachings.

What individual has not experienced this mysterious feeling which makes us retreat into ourselves, all contemplative and dreamy, before the spectacle offered by the sea? In some, depending on their evolutionary degree, a state of admiring stupor takes hold of them, mingled with fear; in others, silent communion invades their inner selves completely.

Each element manifests in its own way the secrets of its deep life. The human soul, by its inner senses, is able to perceive this language. Things tend toward us, without always reaching us. Our soul seeks things, without being able to penetrate them completely, yet it approaches them close enough to feel a kinship that connects us. Hence all these links, multiple and hidden bonds and relations between Nature and ourselves. This fusion with the universal soul is reflected in a rapture of life which penetrates us through all the pores, a rapture which words cannot express. The sea, like the forest, like the mountain, acts upon our psychic life, upon our feelings and thoughts, and through this inner communion, the duality of matter and spirit is suspended for a moment, to blend into the great unity that has generated everything. And then we feel associated with the immense forces of the universe, destined like them, albeit in a different way, to play a role in the vast theater of life.

———

The sea is a great revitalizer. Without it, the earth would be sterile, utterly infertile; in its bosom beneficent rains are produced; the entire irrigation system of the globe is born there. Its outpouring of life is boundless. This great salutary force, albeit harsh and savage, corrects and attenuates our physical and moral weaknesses. Through the perpetual danger it presents, the sea is a school of heroism. It communicates its energies to humans; to their thoughts and characters, it imparts seriousness, introspection, and that particular impression of calm and composure typical of the inhabitants of the coasts. With its life-giving breaths it toughens both bodies and wills, by providing stamina and vigor. Hence the sea has always had its faithful, its lovers, its devotees. In spite of its furies and rages, and constant perils, those who have long sailed it can no longer keep away from it: they are attached to the sea down to the innermost fibers of their being.

The vast sea is for us an image of power, of expanse, of permanence. All who have described the globe have compared it to a living organism; they say they can feel, on certain summer days, its pulsations. The ebb and flow, its breathing. At night, while hearing in the distance the monotonous sound of the waves, I often had the impression that the ocean breathes like a sleeping giant, a leviathan.

Its massive currents radiate heat and electricity to the ends of the Earth. There are on our planet two intense centers of life, namely Java and the Caribbean Sea, surrounded by two circles of volcanoes, huge irradiating cores of vitality and submarine activity. Then two huge rivers come out, like aortas, and warm up the northern hemisphere. The American Matthew Fontaine Maury called them the "two Milky Ways of the Sea."[43] Other secondary streams fertilize the Indian Ocean, bathing a vast network of islands, reefs and benches where the work of polyps lays the foundation of a future continent.

Indeed the sea has its pulsations, but it also has its spasms, its convulsions. However, its true personality is not revealed in the incidents or crises occurring on its surface: the most violent storms only affect a very small part of its liquid mass. To know the sea, one must study it in its mysterious depths. There, eight thousand meters below surface, obscure and strange life forms dwell, made to glow by phenomena of phosphorescence which fill with surreal light the silent night of the abyss.

Luminous beings swarm there. When they are drawn to the surface, they shine for a moment with fiery streaks and shining sprays, only to extinguish them as soon as possible. Their forms are infinitely varied, presenting the most unexpected aspects and colors: cathedral rosettes, strings of pearls and coral, crystal chandeliers with rich girandoles; marine stars tinged with green, purple and azure. Their fleeting apparition is dazzling; it gives us a weak idea of the wonders hidden in the secret vaults of the sea. Then there

---

43 [Trans. note] For L. DENIS's uncredited reference, see J. MICHELET, *The Sea* (London: T. Nelson & Sons, 1875), p. 45, "Maury calls the two warm rivers of India and America the 'two Milky Ways of the Sea.'" *Cf.* Matthew Fontaine MAURY, *The Physical Geography of the Sea* (New ed. New York: Harper & Brothers, 1858), ch. XV, p. 294, "Milky Way of the Sea," par. 848, where MAURY's actual comparison is found.

is the magical vegetation, giant fucus, mothers-of-pearl, brightly colored enamels, forests of corals, gorgonians and irises; a whole singular world, which is the first awakening of life, the effort of a thought aspiring to light. What mysteries are hidden in the depths of this darkness! How many sunken continents and once flourishing cities now lie under the shroud of the immense waters!

This was the gigantic crucible where the first manifestations of life were elaborated. Even today, it is still the birth mother, the fertile nurse through whom prodigious lives are being developed, and whose overflowing sap nor the desperate rage of humans, nor the combined causes of mortality, or the struggle of war between species, in short, absolutely nothing can lessen its intensity. The reproductive capacity of some species is such that, without the forces that fight it and mitigate its effects, the sea would long have become a solid mass.

Herring move in innumerable shoals, with torrents of fertility.[44] Each of them carries an average of fifty thousand eggs, and each egg in turn multiplies by fifty thousand. Cod, which thrive on herring, has nine million eggs, a third of its weight, and it produces nine months out of twelve. Sturgeon, which thrive on cod, are hardly less prolific. Just the three of them, in their eagerness to reproduce, would have succeeded in filling the ocean were it not for the elements of death that come to restore balance. By this means, immolation becomes beneficent, for without the combat among species, harmony would be broken, and life would perish by its own excesses.

As far as the world of the seas is concerned, essential work consists in loving and multiplying! In some regions,

---

[44] On a certain day, near Le Havre (France), says J. MICHELET, a fisherman caught eight hundred thousand fish in his nets. At a port in Scotland they filled eleven thousand barrels in one night. One hundred thousand sailors live exclusively from cod fishing.

when salt water is examined under a microscope, it shows a frightening quantity of eggs, germs, and protozoans. The ocean is like an immense tank of existences still in fermentation, always in birth labor. Death gives birth to life: in the organic debris of destroyed beings, other organisms appear and develop ceaselessly!

XIII

THE MOUNTAIN
(TRAVEL IMPRESSIONS)

At some points on the French coast, sea and mountain meet, facing each other. They oppose each other, this one with the variety of its forms in a silent still landscape, the other full of noise and endless movement in its monotony. On one side, restless agitation; on the other, a majestic calm.

Nature seems to like such contrasts. The mountains, at times rugged and bare, at times adorned with verdure, rise above the deep valleys and vast horizons of the sea; or frame in graceful or austere sites the blue water of the lakes. Above all things, space unfolds, and, in higher up in the skies, the stars pursue their eternal course.

The work is varied in every detail; but, from the various elements which compose it, a powerful harmony emerges, in which the art of its Divine Author is revealed. The same applies to the moral field. There are innumerable souls, with infinitely varied aptitudes: dull or brilliant souls, noble or crude, sad or joyful, souls of faith, souls of doubt, souls of ice, souls of fire! All seem to mingle, mixed-up in the immense arena of life. From these apparent discordances, from these attractions, from these contrasts, come all the struggles, conflicts, hatreds, mad passions, intoxicating felicities, and acute pains. Yet, also from this continuous stirring, a mixture occurs; perpetual exchanges take place; a growing order emerges. The fragments of the rocks, the stones carried by the torrent, are changed in the long run into round and polished pebbles. It is the same for human souls: struck, rolled by the river of successive existences, step by step, from lifetime to lifetime, they move along the path of perfecting themselves.

───

France is admirably endowed with mountains. They cover a third of its territory and, depending on the latitudes and the intensity of the light that bathes their peaks, they offer a marvelous variety of aspects and hues.

In the north-east, the Vosges, with their red sandstone rocks piercing the ground, and old burgs hanging like eagle's nests at the height of the clouds, and dark fir forests lining their flanks.

At the center, the large volcanic massif of Auvergne, with craters invaded by water, giving rise to the famous volcanic *puys* and the extensive *cheires* or lava flows. In the south, there is the bleak and fantastic country of the Causses, with its narrow gorges and red cliffs, its abysses and subterranean rivers.

Serving as a frame for this vast painting, a series of mountains range from the Franche-Comté to Béarn. These are the Jura, the Savoy Alps, the Dauphine and Provençal Alps, the sunny coasts of the blue sea, the Esterel and the Cévennes. Finally, the high wall of the Pyrenees with its serrated peaks, its sublime semicircular basins and romantic solitudes.

All these mountains of France are familiar to me. Very often I have traveled the length of them. I can say that it was one of the rare joys of my life to savor their exhilarating beauties. The mountain is my temple! It keeps me away from the usual ways of this world, and closer to heaven, to God!

With the unexpected turns in its landscape and the unfolding of its enchantments – snowy peaks, dazzling glaciers, formidable escarpments, caves, shady ravines, pastures, lakes, torrents, waterfalls – the mountain is an inexhaustible source of strong impressions, lofty sensations and fruitful lessons.

With unexpected changes in its landscape and the unfolding of its enchantments – snowy peaks, dazzling glaciers, formidable escarpments, caves, shady ravines, pastures, lakes, torrents, waterfalls – the mountain is an inexhaustible source of strong impressions, lofty sensations and fruitful lessons.

How good it is when, at the fresh of dawn, still infused with the penetrating scents of the night, one climbs the slopes, holding a big pointed stick in the hand and carrying a bag of provisions on the shoulder! Around you, everything is calm; the earth exhales that serene peace which reinvigorates the heart and suffuses it with inner joy. The path is so graceful in its outlines, the forest so full of shade and mysterious sweetness! As you climb up, the scenery widens, great vistas open far into the plains. Villages show their white spots in the greenery, among the harvest crops, moors and woods. In ponds and rivers, water sparkles like polished steel.

Soon, the vegetation becomes less dense, the path steeper, covered with tree trunks and fallen blocks. From all sides altitude florets appear: arnica with yellow flowers, rhododendrons, saxifrages, blue and white irises. Balsamic scents float in the air. Everywhere, gushing waters and clear springs. Their murmur fills the mountain with a sweet symphony.

While lying on the moss, I lose count of the hours I spent listening to the crystalline babble of the springs among the rocks, and the voice of the torrent rising in the great silence! Everything reaches an ideal level at these heights.

The distant calls and the melancholy songs of the shepherds, the sound of the cow bells, the roar of the underground waters, the whine of the wind in the larches, everything turns into a melody – but wait! Here comes the storm with its powerful voice silencing all the others!

I love everything about the mountain: its sunny days full of scents and rays of light, and its serene nights under millions of stars that glitter more brightly and seem closer to you. I even like its storms and the bursts of lightning at its summit.

Now the storm has subsided and Nature has resumed its festive air. Everywhere the grinding of locusts and the rattles of crickets can be heard. Insects of all shapes and colors manifest in their own way their exuberant enjoyment of life, of being inebriated with air and light. Further down, in the deep forest, the enchanted forest, there is a concert of beings and things going on, dominated by the low height breeze in the branches: bird songs, buzzing of insects, the sounds of streams, springs and cascades, all of them enchanting, enveloping the listener in an indefinable and irresistible charm.

Let us resume our trail walk. After some effort, panting, you reach the top. Oh, but how rewarding was your trouble! An immense panorama unfolds, an incomparable scenery is suddenly revealed, a spectacle that dazzles the eye and fills the soul with religious emotion.

Peaks and summits rise in the glory of dawn. At the bottom of the horizon, solemn crests line up, all snow white, with their glaciers that the Sun shines on like silver tablecloths. Between their huge tops, wild gorges open up and sweet valleys stretch afar. Toward the north, the mountain chain lowers into soft hills, making way for an endless plain. The last foothills are covered with pretty woods, fresh meadows, picturesque villages. Farther away, a boundless expanse of green carpet and golden fields;

meadows, heathers, moors, a checkerboard of plantations, a variety of hues and colors that melt into a distant vaporous landscape. Farther still, the immense sea shines under the infinite azure.

Time passes fast at these heights. Soon, we must think about the way back. Slowly, the Sun goes down and the valleys are filled with shade. Already the black silhouettes of the great peaks stand high in the pure sky where stellar fires are lit. The torrent's voice arises, louder and more austere in the peaceful evening. The flocks are collected by the shepherds, under the watchful eyes of the dogs. Now bells jingle with silver tones, inviting repose and slumber. The lights go out, one by one, in the entire valley. And my soul, lulled by the harmonies of the mountain, offers an ardent homage to the almighty God, Creator of the whole universe.

Young people who read me, my thoughts go to you with brotherly wishes in order to entreat you: Learn to love the mountain. It is a book par excellence, in front of which every human book is comparatively small. By leafing through its majestic pages, a thousand hidden beauties will appear to you, a thousand revelations which you did not even suspect. You will collect precious joys that can enrich your soul by purifying it. Learn to see, read and hear it. Fill your eyes and your hearts with these agreeable and charming landscapes. Penetrate its grace and strength, its harshness and gentleness. Alternately, the ancient and venerable trees, the rumbling torrents, and the mountain top will teach you sublime lessons, engraved forever in your memory as you cradle sweet memories during sad and dark days of decline later in your life. Learn to understand their language. United, their voices make up the worship hymn that all beings and things sing to the Eternal.

The mountain is like the Bible, I said, whose pages have a hidden and profound meaning. In its rocky layers, folded, circumvented in the abyssal upheavals, you can read the genesis of the whole globe, the great epics of the history of the world before the appearance of humans. The movements of the Earth's crust, written around you in formidable characters, will show you the action of the combined forces which created our collective abode. Then, it will reveal the slow work of the water, drip by drip digging circuses and gorges, and sculpting granite colossi. Finally, it will offer the study of its flora and fauna in their unlimited diversity.

The eruptive flares, the cooled lava flows, the giant porphyries will tell you of the efforts of the burning mass raising mountain chains in sharp jets or rounded domes.

Volcanoes are the respiratory openings of the Earth. One is able to feel very well the violent circulation beneath, the surge of sap and life which, without these outlets, would shake the ground and break the planetary bark. The hot springs show you that the bowels of the globe still conceal ardent, burning and ready-to-gush life – and that the action of this enormous dark Cyclops always remains a latent possibility.

From the central core, from the bottom of the abyss, expansive forces rise up to the surface, transforming the elements by liquefying them and charging them with unknown electric power, in their surge toward the Sun, whose radiations spur and draw them throughout the space.

This is the prodigious laboratory where the great work is elaborated, a preparation of the vast theater where the dramas of life will be played out.

To all those who know how to love it and understand it, the mountain becomes a long and deep initiation.

The flower opens itself to the caresses of the Sun and the dew drops: in the same way, the soul blossoms under great Nature's radiant influence. Under these powerful impressions, everything moves and vibrates within it. It prays, and its prayer is a cry of gratitude and love. From prayer it passes to contemplation, that higher form of thought by which the august meaning, the divine meaning of the universal work, mysteriously penetrates us.

Yet contemplation alone is not enough. Real life is action; the law imposes on us struggle and trials: we can acquire merit only through them. Our duties, our daily tasks absorb us, keeping us away from the pure sources of thought. That is why it is good, it is salutary to turn from time to time toward Nature, to draw from it forces and inspirations. Those who neglect or ignore it diminish themselves. On the other hand, to those who love it, it imparts moral assistance, the additional supplies necessary for one to walk through the rocks and mists of life toward the supreme goal which is bright and distant.

Like the sea, and more than this, the mountain is soothing and invigorating. It possesses a regenerative principle that calms the nerves, restores health; and is a vital means of recovery for our weak human species.

In the mountains, all feverish agitations, all worries of the fictitious, stifling life of cities, vanish to make room for a simpler, more natural way of existence. The altitudes are a school of energy for those whom the city has not enfeebled. In the great outdoors vast perspectives sharpen the eye. Our lungs dilate with the pure air of the summits. Barriers stimulate our efforts; climbing again and again gives us muscles of steel. At the same time that our physical strength unfold, our intellectual powers are also reconstituted, our wills tempered. Thus we hasten to act, to conquer, and to despise death.

For the mountain has its dangers. Its paths are steep, its precipices spooky. Vertigo awaits you at its heights. On certain days, the wind is rough and lightning often strikes. Or sudden mists envelop you, hiding the dangers ahead. Sometimes you have to walk on narrow ledges between the abyss and the avalanche, trying to avoid the gaping crevices of the glaciers, and go down slippery slopes that end in chasms. During my travels, I frequently heard echoes of heavy thunder, falling rocks, or masses of snow. In such and such a wild retreat of the mountains, or a desolate ravine, you suddenly find yourself in presence of crosses that mark the spot where many a traveler has perished.

On the other hand, up there one finds all the inebriating sensations, all the harmonies of light and assorted enchantments unknown to the plains. One perceives a universal mysterious symphony of noises, perfumes and colors, the soft inner music of the breezes and waters. The melancholy of the evening is better appreciated when the smell of meadows and woods, from the bosom of the valleys, rises up to the top. Then, the human soul can break the bonds that bind it to the flesh, and hover in the subtle ether. It then experiences ecstasies almost divine.

It is not without reason that the most important events of religious history have taken place on mountain summits. The Meru Peak in the Himalayas, the Bodh Gaya,[45] Mount Sinai, Mount Nebo, Mount Tabor, the Calvary are all superb altars from which rises, with powerful impetus, the prayer of the great initiators.

In souls of higher degree, the majesty offered by such great spectacles of Nature awakens their innermost senses, psychical faculties, and communion with the Unseen is

---

[45] In India, where Buddha is said to have received enlightenment.

established. But, though at different degrees, almost all of us can feel this influence. At such moments, what is artificial or ordinary in our existence vanishes to give way to superhuman impressions. It is like a clearing, a sunny spell opening in the midst of our darkness, through the black smoke that usually hides the sky and asphyxiates the most beautiful intelligences in the long run. For a moment we are able to glimpse the celestial, infinite higher world. Then radiations of divine thought descend like dew into our delighted souls.

When far away from prejudices and regular social routines, the soul can blossom freely. It finds its own genius, the *awen* (inspiration) of the Druids. Its sure intuitions tell it that all systems are sterile and that only the great mother Nature, the great living book, can teach us truth and perfect beauty. At the hours of deep recollection, when the Sun casts a prodigality of purple upon an assembly of mountains, or when the Moon spreads its silvery light in the midst of absolute silence, a solemn conversation is established between one's soul and God.

Sudden halts in life are indispensable for rediscovering, recognizing, and recovering ourselves; and for seeing and to guiding us with a sure step toward the supreme goal. Then, like the prophets of yore, we come down from the peaks, feeling uplifted and enlightened by an inner light.

A multitude of memories awaken at the call of my thoughts. Now I am in the Pyrenees, ascending to the peak of Ger, near Eaux-Bonnes. To reach the rocky platform, its summit which is a kind of belvedere, one must cross astride a fifty-meter-long ridge, sharp as a razor, which lies above a vertiginous abyss of two thousand feet. But, from there, what a panorama! The whole central chain unfolds from the Mount Maudits to the Peak of Anie, whose black summit emerges from a sea of clouds like an island in the middle of the ocean.

The atmosphere is so pure and limpid that one can distinguish the contours of the most distant mountains. The Vignemale, Neouvielle, the group of great peaks of Bigorre, with their fine ridges and crowns of glaciers and immaculate snow, stand up like white ghosts under the ardent light of the South. Thanks to the transparency of the air, the Spanish peaks, located more than a hundred kilometers away, are so clearly displayed that one might think they are very close.

I can see them as if it were only yesterday, these majestic summits dominating lines of crests which follow one another to the very end of the horizon: the huge Balaitous, and beyond, in an indentation, the dark Mount Perdu. Closer to home there appear the familiar shapes of the Monne, the Gabizos, the gigantic heights of Marboré, the Taillon, and the breach of Roland, like old acquaintances that I greet from afar with great pleasure.

An unalterable serenity envelops this assembly of giants, frozen in an eternal confab. In the foreground, the granite peak of Ossau, solitary and wild, continues its dream lasting hundreds of centuries.

Down there, these reddish mountain tops which spread out to the south belong to the Spanish side of the Pyrenees – rough, devoured by the Sun, but not as rich in color. From this slope, I have explored many times the wild basins, so little known and of difficult access, the Spanish *gargantas* (gorges), chasms where waterfalls leap, and where roaring, untouched streams have hollowed out an underground bed amidst a hellish chaos. And behold! Paths cut in cornices on the flanks of steep walls! Under your feet opens the abyss, several hundred yards deep; over your head, vultures with voracious appetites spin in large circles. Between these jagged crests lies the Bramatuero Cirque, a sinister corridor cut with snow and icy lakes, where an Italian priest, going to Lourdes, was murdered a few days prior to my passage. Farther away, hidden in a funnel cirque, with steep bare walls, there is Panticosa, a resort in Spain. The site is desolate throughout. From the bottom of the gorges rises the roar of the waters, similar to the rumblings of a troop on march or the rolling of wagons.

Let us go back to the peak of Ger. On a nearby glacier, my guide points out to me a motionless black spot, which I took to be a rock. On hearing the guide's cries, the object moves and dislocates itself, escaping quickly. It was a chamois. The shouts of the guide had awakened the echoes of the mountain. From all folds of the ground, from wild ravines and narrow gorges, came out thousands of voices sounding like a legion of goblins, gnomes and mocking spirits. The effect was simply stunning.

Now let us take one last long look at the splendid panorama. Under the azure hill, high mountains are colored with melted hues of incomparable purity and richness. The midday Sun spreads over them a profusion of brightness, a streaming of golden light, increasing even more the prestige of their fantastic and tormented profiles. A whole world of towers, needles, crenelated peaks, domes, pinnacles, and pyramids, stand under the sky, forming a gigantic jumble of lines, sometimes rough and bumpy, sometimes rounded by the slow action of the waters. Scattered in between, there are high green pastures strewn with sheepfolds from which thin threads of bluish smoke rise, and the thick forests bordering the frontier. Toward Gabas,[46] sparkling

---

46 [Trans. note] Located in the valley of the Gave d'Ossau in the French Pyrenees, Gabas is a hamlet in Aquitaine.

cascades, tranquil lakes, laughing meadows and icy pla-
teaus, gloomy deserts of rubble and scree, and ruins of
fallen mountains.

In the presence of this spectacle, all our impressions are
merged into the sensation of immensity. It is a splendor made
of shapes, aspects and colors that cannot be described in
the pale words of earthly language. The human being then
admits its tininess; all its works seem to be ephemeral and
meager next to these colossal structures. A single tremble
or tremor of these latter, would suffice to make all human
work collapse and disappear. Yet the soul grows through
thinking. A world of intuitions and dreams awakens within
our soul. It feels that these great spectacles of Nature are
but mere foretastes of the wonders that destiny holds for us
in our eternal ascension, from orb to orb, in the succession
of times and sidereal worlds.

The whole universe is reflected in us as in a mirror. The
invisible world, through an imperceptible transition, connects with the visible world. Above them a law of harmony
reigns supreme, governing them both. And the soul in its
contemplation is projected out of itself, exteriorized in some
way, penetrating and embracing both of them. For a moment, it can feel the great thrill of the infinite pass through
itself, and thus communicate with the supreme thought. It
then understands that the Creator gave birth to the worlds
only to serve as stations in our spiritual ascension.

~

One evening in July, during a solitary walk around Eaux-
Bonnes, I was lost in the woody mountain of Gourzy. After
night had fallen, making my return impossible through

the steep paths I had followed, I had to resign myself to waiting for the next morning, lying on an makeshift bed made of moss. That night has left in my mind memories full of charm and deep poetic feeling. What impressions have I had! I could hear yelps and calls from the woods: the fox, the grouse, the great owl of the mountains with an almost human cry. Life lurked around me full of mystery; I could hear its rumors and slightest palpitations.

At some distance, in a thicket, a strange illumination caught my attention. I came closer: it was an assembly of glowworms. Their little green lanterns dotted the bushes, while in the sky much more powerful lights were shining above my head. During that night I was able to watch the whole parade of the heavenly army. Then, with that imposing march of the stars, there came the moon, whose trembling light glided through the foliage and came to play on mosses and ferns. No thought of fear disturbed my soul. I felt surrounded by invisible protectors, invaded by a sort of inexpressible bliss. The great voice of the mountain stream could be heard in the night silence, talking of deep and solemn things. What was it saying? It spoke of the aspiration toward the divine; it sang of immortality, the participation of every being according to its measure in the immense work, the powerful harmony of the world. It was saying, "Behold my course; it is the image of your destiny. Once I fled, as impetuous torrent, among tormented blocks. My stream now rolls in cascades or breaks in foam. Yet, later, I will become a broad river, obstructed by islets, and then flow, calm and imposing, through emerald meadows, under an opalescent sky. This is what the momentous voice, superb in its majesty and eloquence, says to me as I contemplate the heavens.

Up there, other problems draw my attention. Where are these innumerable worlds going? By what force do they move, seeking each other within the unfathomable abyss? Always, in the depths of everything, there arises the thought of God, eternal energy, eternal love! The hand that directs the stars in the infinite expanse has written a name in letters of fire – a single name! All these worlds know their way, their sacred mission; they pursue them infallibly. They know that they play a role in the divine plan and are closely associated with it. All the secret of Nature lies there. The seas, the forests, the mountains do not utter anything else. The Milky Way which unrolls its dust of worlds through deep space, the giant cedars which extend their long branches above precipices, the flower which swoons from the kisses of the Sun, all murmur the same to us: it is to God that we must exist; it is for God that we live and die!

Indeed, this is the sanctuary where the soul opens and blossoms at the sight of the great heaven and of God, which created order and sublime beauty. This is the temple of the eternal and living religion, whose inescapable law is written at the forefront of starry nights and in the depths of human consciousness.

But behold, dawn comes with a majestic sunrise on the distant peaks. Like a sphere of red metal, the star-king rises in the horizon. At first, the jagged summits blaze in the resurgent light, and, just as in the prior evening, it rapidly rises around me, with the shadow descending at similar speed. As if a veil had been torn apart, all the details of the forest, its high foliage, the abrupt escarpments of the rocks, the sinuosities of the path, all of a sudden light up. Alluring beauty of most amazing colors! In an instant, everything comes alive, quivers and throbs; sky and earth vibrate with a long shudder. Above the narrow gorge where the mountain stream sings, the black silhouette of the Ossau Peak is clearly outlined. And I walk back to my hotel, blessing the circumstances that allowed me to witness such spectacular displays of Nature.

Other impressions were in store for me in the Alps. One could say with reason that the Pyrenees, because of their agile, slender and elegant shapes, represent the feminine type of mountain. They often possess the charm and grace usually found in women, with a light protective veil enshrouding their superb foreheads. At other times, flickering lights transfigure them, turning them into enchanted mountains.

The Alps, with their massive shapes and more robust framework, are more reminiscent of the masculine type. They symbolize strength, duration, austere grandeur; they look like the gigantic boundaries that mark the frontiers of time and eternity.

On laying eyes on Mont Blanc for the first time – that solitary giant whose summit dominates Europe – one feels as if crushed before its immense shroud-like whiteness. Indeed, its appearance reminds one of death. And yet, under its thick cloak made of snow, hides a life always active, always hot and dazzling, which is manifested and poured out through the bubbling springs of the French resort of Saint-Gervais-les-Bains.

Add to these 125 square miles of glaciers crowning the Alps with their vast underground reservoirs, which give birth to the greatest rivers of Western Europe, while pouring fertility over so many plains, and you will have a glimpse of this formidable chain.

In the massif of Oisans, the sensation is no less intense than at Mont Blanc. From the belvedere of the Tête de la Maye, you can see a whole forest of sharp peaks and pinnacles, forming an edge indentation made of granite. The day I went up, the glaciers were shining, melting slowly under the heat of the Sun; streams and cascades flowed from all sides. The rolling of the water rushing under the ground, produced a dull sound which varied from hour to hour, according to the volume of the liquid mass. Around me, the place was desert: as far as one's sight could reach, not a single human being. The imposing silence of the summits enveloped me. I could hear only the roar of the waters and the lament of the wind waving the Alpine grasses and flowers. A wonderful flora spreads on these heights. Here is the edelweiss and the thistle with its frail stem. Bellflowers swing their graceful bells. Further away is the blue gentian bordered in black, and so haughty in its attitude; then there is the superb yellow anemone, so much sought after by botanists. Then behold the daphne, the orchis, the foxglove, twenty species whose names I know not. In a word, a whole small vegetable world blossoms under this sky of fire. And the air is ever so balmy.

Blocking the horizon, the peak called La Meije, a formidable "man-eating" mountain, shows its powerful buttresses prevailing over a diadem of snow and ice. Mount Pelvoux and the Barre des Écrins, among other summits, rise like a family of titans arranged in a semicircle.

Now, behold, this is the mountain monastery of La Grande Chartreuse. I spent several days in this haven of peace and meditation. I explored its surroundings by walking under the dark vaults of the forest that surrounds it, while listening to the song of the torrents and the great pipe organs of the wind that blew through the branches, and the distant calls of the herdsmen and lumberjacks. The bell tolls the monastery reached me on the wing of a breeze; their vibrations in sound waves would die and be reborn, then lose themselves at the bottom of the gorges and on the slopes of the mountain. On all sides the view is surrounded by tall, bald, rough and bare summits, beaten with storms. But the thought of the absolute and the infinite surrounds these mountains; and God's gaze hovers over all things.

In the great silence of the cloister, the clock slowly strikes the hours. So many souls shaken by the storms of life have come here to seek repose and forgetfulness! The Christian mysticism that attracted them has profound depths which fascinate. No doubt, it goes astray in many ways, moving away from unseen realities. It creates in the brain of the believer a whole world of illusions and superstitious chimeras imposed by the tyranny of dogmatists. Yet it is not totally devoid of beauty. In times of iron and blood, monastic life was the only refuge for delicate and studious souls. Even in modern times, it could become to a certain extent a means of training toward loftier goals, a preparation for the Hereafter. That is why, from this Alpine sanctuary, the whole country once radiated beneficent influences. Since then, the monks have disappeared, the Chartreuse has been abandoned; the site has lost its religious prestige.

From the visitors' gallery, I attended the midnight service. Three faint lights, spaced in the nave of the chapel, alone pierced the deep darkness. The Carthusians[47] arrived one by one, each carrying a little lantern, and moved on to their stalls. The psalmodies began together with invocations and cries of appeal of souls in distress: *Deus in adjutorium meum intende!* ("Make haste, O God, to deliver me! LORD, make haste to help me!" Ps 70:1)

This sorrowful lament by Job, which has passed through the centuries, seems to sum up all human suffering. It is the complaint of all broken hearts, of all those who

---

[47] [Trans. note] *Carthusians* were monks or nuns of an austere contemplative order founded by St. Bruno in 1084.

have dissociated themselves from this land of trials –
where they see nothing but despair, abandon and exile
– so as to seek help and consolation in the bosom of our
Divine Parent.

These austere monks, who left their hardships to join
in thought with suffering humanity, and these chants of
poignant sadness, which resound when everything else is
asleep, are all very moving.

Psalms follow one another other in a slow, serious,
and solemn rhythm. From these melancholy, sometimes
monotonous notes, rises, from time to time, a cry of love,
a veritable flower of the soul which, from this ocean of
human miseries, ascends to heaven to beseech the Creator.
Then the chanted sentences subside. In the dim light of the
stalls, the prostrate monks seem to be immersed in deep
meditation. Finally, David's last exhortation to penitence
bursts forth, like the ultimate sob of a torn humanity, which
a ray of hope comes to enlighten and warm: *De profundis
clamavi ad te, Domine, exaudi vocem meam!* ("Out of the
depths I cry to you, O LORD! O Lord, hear my voice!"
Ps 130:1)

The cemetery of the convent is gloomy. No slab, no
inscription marking the graves. In the gaping pit, one
simply deposits the body of the Carthusian monk, clad
in his coat and nailed to a board, without a coffin; then,
it is covered with earth. No other sign than a cross des-
ignates the sepulcher of this passerby of life, this host of
silence, of whom no one, except the prior, will know the
true name!

Is this the first time I have walked through those long
corridors and lonely cloisters? Certainly not.

When I search my past, I feel the mysterious chain that
connects my present personality to that of past centuries. I
know that among the remains that lie there, in this cemetery,
there is one that my spirit once animated. I have had a

formidable privilege, that of knowing my past lives. One of them ended in these places. After twenty years of struggles in the Napoleonic era, in which fate had thrown me, tired of everything, disgusted by the sight of blood and smoke of so many battles, I came here to seek deep peace. In the series of one's successive lives, a monastic existence can be useful, if it teaches us the detachment from worldly things, the concentration of thought, the austerity of manners. In the cloister, the spirit is free from material influences and thus open to divine visions!

Would it not be good if all souls descended into the flesh retaining the memory of their previous lives? I do not think so. God has wisely veiled to our eyes, at least during the difficult passage of earthly life, all tragic scenes, our failures, and fatal errors committed in our distant past.

Pressure is thus eased off our present, our current tasks are made easier. It would always be too soon if, after returning to the spiritual plane, we immediately saw accusing ghosts standing before us. No doubt many individuals have nothing of the kind to fear. May peace be in your spirit! As for me, I know one thing: when I leave Earth to return to the Hereafter, voices of the past will certainly wake up and shout against me, for I was a culprit, and blood once reddened my hands. Yet I hope the souls that I have been able to enlighten and comfort in this lifetime will also rise up to plead on my behalf, somehow attenuating the supreme judgment.

XIV

ᴇLEVATION

S pirit, soul, you who are leafing through these pages: Where do you come from? Where are you going to? You have been ascending from the depths of the abyss, while climbing the innumerable steps of the ladder of life. You are heading for the eternal homes where the Great Law calls, and where God's hand leads. You are going to the Light, to absolute Wisdom and Beauty!

Contemplate and meditate! Everywhere, beautiful and powerful works beckon your attention. By studying them, you will draw, with courage and confidence, the right feeling of your own value and future. Humans do not hate each other, they only despise themselves because they ignore the magnificent order by which they all have been brought close together.

Your pathway is immense; yet the final goal surpasses in splendor all that you can possibly conceive. Now you may look very small in the middle of the colossal universe; but you are great in thought, great in your immortal destiny.

Work, love and pray! Cultivate your intelligence and your heart! Develop your consciousness make your awareness larger and more sensitive. Each lifetime is a fertile crucible, from which you must get out purified, ready for future missions, ripe for ever-more noble and greater tasks. Thus, from sphere to sphere, from circle to circle, you will pursue your course, acquiring new strengths and faculties, united to the beings you have loved, those who have lived and will live with you.

You will evolve in common with them on the spiral of existences, amidst unsuspected marvels, because the universe, like yourself, develops through work and unfolds its living metamorphoses, offering new joys and ever increasing satisfactions, always renewed with aspirations geared toward the pure desires of the spirit!

In hours of hesitation, turn to Nature: it is the great inspirer, the august temple where, under its mysterious veils, the hidden God speaks in the heart of the wise, in the mind of thinkers. Behold the deep firmament: the stars that populate it are stages of your long pilgrimage, stations of the great path where your destiny is carrying you.

Come! Let us elevate our souls; hover for a moment with me, by thought, among suns and worlds! Higher, ever higher in the unfathomable ether! There, the Earth is only a point in the vast expanse. In front and above us, stars multiply. Everywhere, golden spheres, emerald, sapphire, amethyst and turquoise fires perform rhythmic movements. Toward us there comes a huge star, dragging a hundred planetary worlds into its orbit, a hundred worlds describing perfect ellipses. Here it comes, and we can barely glimpse it; here this moment, gone the next; as it continues its race, along with its splendid retinue.[48] After them, we encounter ten suns of different colors, all grouped in one same luminous atmosphere which envelops them like a glorious scarf.

And endlessly, systems succeed systems, like paradises or floating galleys, magic worlds draped with azure, gold

---

[48] The stars, which their remoteness makes them appear motionless, move in all directions, according to scarcely known laws. Great movements carry each sidereal focus into the infinite whirlpool. Our solar system flies at great speed to the constellation of Hercules and in 65,000 years travels a distance equal to that which separates us from the nearest star, the Alpha Centauri. Our central star is only one of the most modest suns: Canopus surpasses it more than 10,000 times in brilliance, Arcturus 8,000 times. Seen from their surfaces, our dazzling Sun would be an imperceptible dot in deep space.

and bright light. Farther on we find the vagabond comets, the pale nebulae of which every atom is a sun still in the cradle.[49] Know one thing: all these worlds are homes to other societies of souls. Even in distant stars, whose tremulous glimmers take thousands of years to reach us, everywhere the human family extends its empire; everywhere we have celestial siblings. All these dwellings are destined to be known and enjoyed by us. We will live again on these lands of space, in new bodies, so as to acquire new strengths, further knowledge and greater merits, and to elevate ourselves even higher in our perpetual journey.

So many worlds, so many schools for the soul; so many fields of evolution to expand our knowledge and, at the same time, to build us fluidic organisms that are more and more delicate, refined and brilliant. After the struggles, the torments, and the setbacks of a thousand arduous existences, after the trials and pains of different planetary

---

[49] According to telescopic observations and space photography, science has established that our universe consists of a billion stars. C. FLAMMARION believes that this universe is not unique. Nothing, he says, proves that this billion exists alone in the infinite and that, for example, there is not a second, a third, a fourth, or a hundred or a thousand universes similar to the others. These universes can be separated by absolutely empty spaces, devoid of ether and, consequently, invisible to each other. It even seems that we already found stars that do not belong to our sidereal universe. We can cite, for example, with NEWCOMBÉ, the star #1830 of GROOMBRIDGE's catalog, the fastest of which had its movement determined. Its speed is estimated to be 320,000 meters per second, and the attractive force of our entire universe could not have determined such a speed. In all probability, this star comes from outside and crosses our universe like a projectile. The same can be said of #9352 of LACAILLE's catalog; and even of the star Arcturus, the fourth in size of all visible stars; and of Mu Cassiopeia (Conference, August 1906). Allow me to add that the powers of Nature are limitless, in both extent and duration. Light, which travels at 300,000 kilometers per second, takes 20,000 years to cross the Milky Way, an tiny anthill of stars of which we are part. These families or nebulae are innumerable and new ones are discovered every day, for example the second of Orion, whose extent frightens the imagination. We live in an absolute without limits, without a beginning or an end.

cycles, there come centuries of happiness living on these happy stars whose softened brightness projects rays of peace and joy onto us. Then, the blessed missions, the noble apostleship, the envied task of causing the awakening and blossoming of sleeping souls, by helping, in our turn, our younger siblings in their wanderings through material regions.

Finally, we reach the sublime depths, a heaven of ecstasy where divine thought vibrates more powerful and melodious; where time and distance vanish; where light and love join their radiations; where the cause of causes, in its incessant fecundity, eternally gives birth to everlasting life and beauty!

Nowadays, the sky can no longer be what human science once thought it to be, namely, a dreary and deserted empty space. We now know that the infinite regularly transforms and animates itself. The circle of our life is expanding in all directions. We feel connected to this universe by a thousand links. Its life is our own; its history our history. Unknown sources of sensation and meditation have been opening up. The future takes on a different character. A deep impression invades us at the thought of such ample destinies. Forever we are united to all that lives, loves and suffers. From all corners of space, from all these stars that shine in the expanse, depart voices that call us, voices of our elder siblings telling us: "Walk, keep walking, get up for the work; do good; accomplish your duty. Come to us who, like you, have toiled, struggled, suffered on the material worlds. Come, continue with us your ascension to God!"

———

Majestic spaces, allow us to look back on Earth. As we know, in spite of its modest proportions, it has its charms and beauty. Each site has its own poetry, each landscape its expression, each valley its particular meaning. Variety is as great in the meadows of our world as in the starry fields.

Summer is the smile of God! Nothing is more sweet and exhilarating than the apotheosis of a beautiful day when all is endearment, sweetness and light. The florets hidden in the grass, the fish that leap in the water in the Sun, with their shimmering silver scales; the birds that sing their notes from the top of the branches; the murmur of the springs; the mysterious song of poplar and elm trees; the wild perfume of the heather moors; all these cradle one's thought and rejoice one's heart. Far from the cities, one finds a deep calm that penetrates the soul, resting it from the struggles and disappointments of life. Only then can one understand the truth of these great words: "Noise is to humans, silence is to God!"[50]

Contemplation and meditation trigger the awakening of our psychical faculties, and through them, an invisible world opens up to our perceptions. I have tried, throughout this book, to express the sensations I felt from the top of altitudes or deep in the seas; to describe the charm of twilights and dawns, the serenity of the fields under the kingly splendor of the Sun, the prodigious poem of starry nights, the magic of moonlight, the enigma of water and wood. There are moments of ecstasy in which the soul can rise out of its envelope and embrace the infinite, moments of intuition and enthusiasm where the divine influx invades us with irresistible force, like a flood; where the supreme thought vibrates and throbs within us, making a ray of genius fleetingly shine. Unforgettable hours sometimes lived by me; and at each of them, I firmly believe to have been visited, and be thoroughly penetrated with the Spirit.

---

[50] [Trans. note] Possibly paraphrased from Saint Amun (also referred to as Ammonius the Hermit), a 4th-century Christian ascetic and monk.

I owe them the inspiration to my most beautiful pages and best public talks.

Those who recollect themselves in silence and solitude, when witnessing the spectacles of the sea or the mountains, feel the birth, the rise, and the growth within them of images, thoughts and harmonies that delight, enchant and console them for their earthly miseries, also opening to them perspectives of the higher life. They understand that God's thought envelops and penetrates everyone when, far from social turpitudes, we become able to open our souls and our hearts to It.

~

Certainly, one could raise many objections. For example, I am often told: "You highlight the beauties of Nature, yet never mentions its uglinesses. Nature is not only made of smiles and caresses: it also has its rebellions, its anger and fury. You never talk about the monsters or the plagues that disfigure it. What use do you find to the existence of beasts of prey, reptiles, and poisonous plants? Why do we have too face convulsions of the soil, disasters, epidemics, and all the evils that cause human suffering?"

Now, that is an easy question for me to answer. Beauty, I would like to stress, requires contrasts. All artists, thinkers and writers of value know that. And when we discover that, among all other worlds, Earth occupies one of the lowest ranks, being suitable, above all, to young spirits, like a school, a place of struggle, of trials and sometimes atonements, how can we be surprised that it is not endowed with all the advantages possessed by higher worlds?

The dangers, the obstacles and difficulties of all kinds are essential factors for our progress, so many spurs that stimulate humans on their path, so many causes that compels one to observe, to be inventive, to provide for or against in advance, to be cautious in one's actions. It is in the mandatory alternation of pleasure and pain that lies the principle of the education souls. Hence the need for all beings, from the most rudimentary to the most developed, to struggle and suffer. Progress cannot be achieved without a necessary balance of opposing feelings, joys and sorrows, which alternate in the grandiose rhythm of life. But it is above all pain, both physical and moral, that forms our experience: human wisdom is its reward.

As for seismic movements, storms and floods, note that they have their laws. It is enough to know these laws in order to foresee and mitigate their effects. When one studies the phenomena of Nature and goes to the depths of things, one promptly recognizes this: what may be an evil in appearance turns out to be a blessing in disguise.[51]

The greatness of the human spirit consists in rising from the confusion, from the chaos of contingencies, to the conception of general order. The spirit can then feel secure in the midst of the perils of the world, because it has understood the great laws which, even at some sacrifice to itself, ensure the balance of life and the salvation of the human race.

The human individual in whom the deep sense, the sensing of divine things, is not awake yet; in a word, the skeptic, whatever the degree of his or her intelligence and knowledge in other matters, refuses to admit such facts. It would be as superfluous to insist on them as to explain to a blind man sunsets and auroras, the play of light on the water or on the glaciers. Such an individual will inevitably need the shocks of adversity, a combination of painful circumstances that will put him or her in direct contact

51 See L. DENIS, *After Death* (Trans. G. G. Fleurot, J. Korngold. New York: USSF, 2017), ch. IX.

with their destiny, and make them feel, together with the usefulness of suffering, these notions of self-sacrifice and hope through which life takes on a real meaning, full of elevation.

From that moment on, one's life, no matter how dull, banal, or colorless it may be, becomes illuminated by a ray of light and poetry; for the truest poetry is made of an inner resonance of the eternal symphony in us, together with the harmony of our thoughts, our feelings and our actions, with the rule of our destiny.

Speaking the way I have done in these pages, I will no doubt be accused of mysticism by a few. But all those whose sensibility and judgment have awakened and developed under the stress of the trials and struggles of existence, will certainly understand me.

Some down-to-earth spirits are inclined to call mystics, lunatics and visionaries, all the individuals whose perceptions go beyond the limited circle of their usual thoughts. They think they are very positive and practical people, whereas in reality only evolved souls, freed from prejudices and passions, disdainful of petty material interests, alone intuit the great and high realities of life. Such higher realities, in the dim light maintained by human conventions, routines and the day-by-day of social life, still escape average people.

In short, Nature and our soul are siblings, with the difference that one invariably evolves according to an established plan, whereas the other traces on a blank page the outlines of its own destiny. They are siblings, for both come from the same eternal cause and are united by a thousand bonds. This explains the empire of Nature over us. It acts on sentient souls like a magnetizer on its subject, causing the spirit to come out of its flesh chrysalis. Then, in the fullness of its psychical faculties, the soul perceives a superior divine world still elusive to most thinking beings.

There is one thing we should never forget: everything that falls within the physical senses, everything that is material, is transient and subject to destruction and to death. Deeper, eternal realities belong to the world of causes, to the realm of the invisible. We ourselves belong to the latter through the imperishable part of ourselves.

Then, little by little, psychical experimentation and its discoveries expand and are made known. The knowledge of the double fluidic body of humans with its action at a distance before and after death; the application of magnetic forces; the appearance on the scene of invisible powers; all of them demonstrate to every attentive observer that the world of the senses is only a poor and obscure prison, compared to the vast and radiant domain open to the spirit.[52]

The inner senses and deep faculties of the soul lie still dormant in most individuals, who are totally oblivious of their hidden riches, their latent powers. That is why their actions lack a basis, a point of support. Hence so many weaknesses and failures. But the time to wake up is near. Every human being will know his or her own time, according to their individual powers and attributes: from then on, separation and death will cease to exist for each one of them; most of the miseries that besiege them will vanish. Our spirit friends will come more often and easily to visit and communicate with us. In time, communion will be established between Heaven and Earth, and

---

[52] See supplemental notes nos. 4, 5 and 6, at the end of this book. Also refer to Léon DENIS, *Into the Unseen* (Trans. H. M. Monteiro. New York: USSF, 2017).

humanity will enter a higher and more beautiful phase of its glorious destiny.

~~~~~

Before finishing this book, with my sight weakened by work, I cast a glance again upon those heavens that call me and this Nature, so intensely loved. I salute the worlds which will later become your and my reward: Jupiter, Sirius, Orion, the Pleiads, and those myriads of orbs whose trembling rays have so often shed serene peace and ineffable comfort into my anxious soul.

Then, from space, I will look back on this Earth which was my cradle and will be my grave. O Earth! Planet, our parent; field of our common labors, of our progress, of our sufferings; where slowly, through the obscurity of the ages, my conscience is hatched with the conscience of the whole humanity; you float in the infinite, cradled by divine breaths; you spread around you powerful vibrations of life which agitates on your flanks. It all sounds like a confused harmony made of rumors and wails, a harmony that rises from the bosom of the seas and continents, valleys and forests, rivers and woods, into which human complaints mingle: a murmur of passions, accents of pain, sounds of work and festive chants, shouts of fury and clangs of armor. Sometimes quiet and serious notes also dominate these noises: human melody replaces the harmonies of Nature and the sound of forces in action; the song of the spirit, freed from lower servitudes, salutes the light. A song of hope goes up to God like a hosanna, a lofty prayer.

It is your soul, O Earth! which, like precious ore, wakes up and makes an effort to get out of its unwanted maze, and mix its radiance and its voice with the radiations and harmonies of sidereal worlds. It is your soul that sings the reborn dawn of humanity that thrives on you; because humans awaken in their turn, leaving their material night, the abyss of their origins. The soul of humanity, which is that of the Earth, seeks itself; it learns to know itself, to penetrate its reason for being; it presses on its great destinies, for it wishes to accomplish them.

Pursue your path, my beloved Earth! Many times already, my spirit has drawn from your elements the bodily forms necessary for its evolution. For centuries, ignorant and barbarous I traveled your trails and forests, and sailed on your oceans, knowing none of the essential things, nothing of the goal to reach.

But now, having arrived at the evening of life, at the twilight hour when another lifetime is coming to an end, and where shadows rise, one bigger than the last, covering all things with their melancholy veil, I ponder over the road I have traveled. Then I direct my eyes forward to the exit that will open to me in the afterlife, and its eternal clarity.

At this hour when my soul is gradually emerging from your shackles, O Earth! – and ready to leave you, it understands the purpose and the law of life. Conscious of your role and my own, grateful for your many benefits, knowing why I am, why I act and how to act, I bless you, O planet Earth! For all the joys and pains, for the salutary trials you have given me, and in all that I owe to you – sensations, emotions, pleasures, sufferings – I recognize the instruments of my education, of my elevation. I bless you and I love you, when I leave you, happily at the thought of coming back later, in a new existence, to work again, to suffer, to perfect myself with you, to contribute with my efforts to your progress and to that of my siblings, who are also your children.

PART THREE

THE CIRCULAR LAW
—
MISSION OF THE 20TH CENTURY

XV

THE CIRCULAR LAW · LIFE
AGES OF LIFE · DEATH

The circular law[53] presides over all the movements of the globe; it governs the evolutions of Nature, those of history and of humanity. Each being gravitates in a circle, each life describes a circuit, all human history is divided into cycles.

The days, the hours, the years, the centuries, all roll in the orbit of space and time and are reborn, since their end is no other than precisely to return to their principle. The winds, the clouds, the waters, the flowers, the light, all follow the same law. The winds return to their orbs entwined with the mysterious caverns from which they proceed.

Steam goes up to the heights where it forms clouds, veritable oceans hanging over our heads. Clouds that hover, like huge and mobile seas, and them melt, raining over the soil and becoming rivers again – rivers that they have already been. Thus the Rhine, the Rhone, the Danube, the Volga have rolled over our heads before sinking at our feet. This is therefore a law, the law of Nature and that of humanity. Every being has already existed; it is reborn and rises, evolving in a spiral, into ever larger orbits, and that is why history takes on an increasingly universal character: it is the law of *corso-ricorso* (the eternal return), as proposed by the Italian philosopher Giambattista Vico (1668–1744).

---

[53] [Trans. note] The *circular law* as described above by Léon DENIS, largely based on G. VICO's ideas, should not be confused with the homonymous law used, for example, in contemporary statistics.

Having laid down these general principles, I now would
like to devote a few pages of this meditation to the study
of the different ages of human life, namely: youth, maturity
and old age, in the light of this great law – with death as
their crowning and apotheosis. From these studies will
emerge the great spiritual principle of reincarnation, the
only one capable of explaining the mystery of our being
and its destiny.

It is necessary to be born again, it is the common law
of human destiny which itself also evolves in a circle of
which God is the center.

"Truly, truly, I say to you, unless one is born again he
cannot see the kingdom of God." And, "Truly, truly, I say to
you, unless one is born of water and the Spirit, he cannot
enter the kingdom of God," said Jesus to Nicodemus.[54]

Reincarnation is clearly expressed in these words, and
Jesus reproaches Nicodemus: "Are you the teacher of Israel
and yet you do not understand these things?"[55]

How many of our contemporary masters deserve the
same reproach! There are so many people who are content
with a superficial notion of life and are never tempted to
look deep inside, in the bottom! It is so easy to deny things
so as to exonerate yourself from the duty and work of
studying and understanding them! Positivist never address
the problem of origins or ends; they are content with the
current moment, and exploit it as best they can. Many
individuals, even very clever ones, do exactly like them. The
Catholic, on the other hand, confine themselves to believing
what the Church teaches, namely, that the beginning and
the end of life are both mysteries, with a few miracles in the
middle – and when these two words are uttered: "miracle,
mystery!" – most people bow, shut up and just accept it.

---

[54] Jn 3:3,5
[55] Jn: 3:10

On the other hand, for a long time scientists and scholars have only believed in data obtained through experimentation. For them, anything that was not included in their program was worthless. Never before did Bacon's idols have more worshipers. Thus, official science has brought but little progress in modern thought in the past fifty years.[56]

However, the physician of our day, lately so attached to the systems of the materialistic school, are starting to shake off that yoke; and it is from the ranks of modern medicine that the most authoritative and best-informed doctors of Spiritualism have emerged.

The next generation will certainly be happier and better endowed. A youth is growing up which does not belong to any academic and is educated only in the great School of Nature and Inner Consciousness. This one will really be a free youth, that is to say, independent from any factitious education, from any empirical and conventional method. Instead, it listens to the real voices; the inner voice, the subliminal voice of being, the one that explains humans to humans and resolves as clearly as possible the theorem of destiny.

It is for this youth of tomorrow that I write these pages; I dedicate them to the "initiates" and the "aware and conscious," to all those who, according to the words of the Master, have eyes to see and ears to hear.

Let us now return to the circular law of life and destiny, that is to say, to the precept of reincarnation.

I briefly summarized the scientific view on the subject, for my aim here is not to write a dogmatic book, but only to abandon myself to Platonic effusions on life, its phases; on destiny, and on death which ends it apparently, to allow it to resume its course.

---

[56] [Trans. note] The 50 years in question lie within 1870–1920.

Birth — The union of soul and body begins at conception and is complete only at the moment of birth. It is the
fluidic envelope (the perispirit) that attaches the spirit to
the embryo; this union becomes ever tighter until it is complete, that is, when the child is born. In the interval from
conception to birth, the faculties of the soul are gradually
annihilated by the ever increasing power of the vital force
received from the biological parents, which diminishes
the vibratory movement of the perispirit until the point
where the child's spirit becomes completely unconscious.
This vibrational lessening of the fluidic movement causes
the loss of memory of past lives, of which I will speak
further below.

A child's spirit thus slumbers in its material envelope,
and as the moment of birth approaches, the spirit's ideas
fade away, as well as the knowledge of the past, of which
it is no longer conscious when the child has reached
the light of day. It will only be when, at the moment
of final dematerialization or by profound influences of
exteriorization through hypnosis, the soul resumes its
vibrational movement, that its past and the world asleep
of its memories will again be retrieved. This is the true
genesis of human life. The achievements of the past are
latent in each soul; its faculties are never lost or destroyed;
they have their roots in the unconscious and are all the
more apparent as they have progressed further before, thus
acquiring even more data, impressions, images, knowledge
and experience. This is what constitutes the "character"
of each living individual and gives him or her its original
abilities proportionate to their degree of evolution.

The child, therefore, owes only one thing to biological
parents: the vital force, to which certain hereditary elements

are also added. At the moment of the spirit's incarnation, the perispirit bonds, molecule by molecule, with the matter of the embryo. In this seed, which must later constitute the individual, resides an initial power which results from the sum of the life elements of the father and the mother, at the moment of conception. This embryo contains greater or lesser potential energy which, by transforming itself into active energy throughout the total duration of a lifetime, determines a being's degree of longevity.

Therefore it is under the influence of this vital force emanating from the biological parents, who themselves inherited it from their ancestors, that one's perispirit develops its functional properties. Thus, the fluidic double replicates in the form of movements the indelible trace of all the states of the soul since its first birth; whereas, the material embryo receives the imprint of all the successive states of the perispirit: here lies a vital parallelism which is absolutely logical and harmonious. The perispirit thus becomes the regulator and support of the vital energy modified through heredity. Thereby the individual type of each of us is formed. This is none other than the "plastic mediator" of British philosophical poet William Wordsworth, that is, the permanent fluidic network through which flows a stream of matter which constantly destroys and reconstructs the living organism. It is the invisible frame that supports the human physical structure internally.

The perispirit is the principle of physical and moral identity which keeps alive, in the midst of vicissitudes suffered by the mobile and changeable being, the principle of the conscious self. The memory which maintains the inner certainty of our personal identity, our *self*, is a reflex radiation of our perispirit.

This is the origin of our life.

Actually, we are only children of ourselves. Facts are there to confirm this assertion. Philosophers of the 18th century, with their concept of the soul similar to a clean slate on which nothing was written yet, have thus been debunked. Doctors of generationism (i.e., traducianism)[57] would be closer to the truth; however, they exaggerated the scope of their tenets and their conclusions.

Undoubtedly, with each reincarnation new modalities are brought into the soul of the child who resumes life through the perispirit, but already finds a cultivated ground for it. Plato was right when he said: "To learn is to remember."

This explains the illustrious phenomena and the physiology found in great geniuses of whom history speaks: the dominant science of Italian philosopher Giovanni Pico della Mirandola; the intuition of French philosopher and mathematician Blaise Pascal, reconstructing at the age of thirteen the theorems of Euclid; and the Austrian composer Wolfgang Amadeus Mozart, who at the tender age of twelve wrote one of his most famous music pieces.

On the other hand however, it may happen that the laws of heredity poses an obstacle to the manifestation of genius, for although the spirit shapes its body, it can only use the elements put at its disposal by its physical inheritance.

For the time being, what I have just said should suffice to scientifically justify the luminous tenet of successive lives (i.e., Spiritism).

We hope to have replied in a few words to the objection of those who keep saying that if our lives were multiple, we would keep at least a vague memory of them.

We have seen above how and why, at the moment of birth, the memory of our past is lost. This partial and momentary eclipse of our former lives is absolutely necessary to preserve intact our freedom down here. If we remembered too easily, there would be confusion in the logical and

---

57 [Trans. note] In Theology, *generationism* (*traducianism*) is the belief that not only the body but also the soul of a child is reproduced by the parents.

inevitable order of destiny; and did the Master not say in his Gospel, "Woe to him who, having put his hand to the plow, looks back." (*Cf.* Lk 9:62)

To draw a straight and safe track, one must look ahead and focus only on the future. However, the obliteration of the past is neither absolute nor definitive. The perispirit, which has recorded all our knowledge, all our sensations, all our acts, awakes under the influence of hypnotism, and the deep voices of the past are again heard. We are like the millennial trees of our forests. Their years are inscribed in the concentric circles of their ages-old bark. Thus, each age of our successive existences leaves an unalterable zone in the perispirit, which faithfully registers the most imperceptible nuances of our past and the most apparently effaced acts of our mental life and our consciousness.

But it is especially at the hour of death that the perispirit, about to disengage from the body, feels the dormant visions of past lives awaken in its memory. The experience of each day attests it. We heard from a friend of mine, a doctor, that in his youth, when he was about to drown, at the very moment when asphyxiation began, all the scenes of his life unfolded before his thinking in retrograde succession, in extremely precise detail and accompanied by a feeling of good or bad from each act of his whole lifetime. It was the spiritual judgment that was thus beginning. This judgment, as we know, is none other than the instantaneous assessment made by our consciousness, which makes us pronounce the verdict on ourselves, thus fixing our fate in the new world, the spiritual world to which we are returning.

Now that we know the law of existence, the scientific principle which lies in reincarnation, it will be easier for us to understand the vicissitudes of our earthly journey, the ages through which we must pass, and the role that each stage of human life comes to play in the harmonious economy of the whole. Thus, youth, mature age, old age, all appear to us under a true perspective; under this high light of Spiritualism, we shall become better able to appreciate and understand them. To die to live again, to live again to die, and to live again and again, such is the unique and universal law. Birth and death are therefore only the luminous or obscure porches under which we must pass in order to enter the temple of our destiny.

Strange thing! This profound knowledge of the origin of things, this genesis of the self, this law of destiny – antiquity knew about them, understood them infinitely better than we do. What we are just beginning to reestablish, and prove scientifically, was already known by Greece, Egypt, and the East through intuition and initiation.

It was the basis of the mysteries of Eleusis and Isis, a sort of dramatic representation of the reincarnation of souls, of their entry into Hades, of their successive purification and transmigration. These festivals lasted three days and translated into a moving trilogy all the mystery of this world and that of the hereafter. At the end of these solemn initiations, the initiates were sacred for the whole of their lives, and the populace who were only served with the symbolism and the hieroglyphs of these esoteric truths felt them under the appearance of the symbol and thus kept the true meaning of life. Today that sense is lost. Primitive Christianity, that of Jesus and the Apostles, still possessed it. From the day when the Greek genius, in its subtlety, created theology, the esoteric sense has disappeared and the secret virtue of the hieratic rites has evaporated like salt turned tasteless. Scholasticism[58] stifled the first revelation under its mountains of specious and sophisticated syllogisms and arguments.

---

[58] [Trans. note] *Scholasticism* was the prevalent system of theology and philosophy taught in medieval Europe.

Pagan mythology was aware of the origins and had the notion of life's genesis in the highest degree. In the form of poetic myths, initiatory truth transpired like the bark of a tree yields the sap of life.

———

It is in the light of New Spiritualism (Spiritism) that I want to study the various phases of human life, connecting them and comparing them to the alternating seasons that follow one another in time.

Like Maurice de Guérin,[59] this well-informed initiate, who died young, as well as all those who "are loved by the gods," we also would like to be able to "penetrate the inner elements of things, to bring up the rays of the stars, and the current of rivers, and that of life, even within the mysteries of their generation; to be finally admitted by the grand Nature in the more withdrawn regions of its divine dwelling places; in other words, to the point of departure of universal life. There, we would certainly witness the first cause of the movement, and hear the first song, of all beings in their morning freshness."[60]

These intuitive gifts are, in some human beings, one of the highest forms of mediumship; for it can be said that mediumship, one in principle and manifold in its manifestations, is the true inner initiation, the mysterious language that the upper world uses to communicate with the soul and the thought of those whom it has elected as its transmitters here below.

Let us therefore meditate, in this light and with such disposition, on the mystery of human life and on the secret

---

[59] [Trans. note] French poet Georges-Maurice de GUÉRIN (1810–1839).

[60] [Trans. note] M. de GUÉRIN, *Journal, lettres, poèmes et fragments* (Strasbourg: Heitz, 1850), p. 98. Excerpt trans. H.M.M.

harmonies which preside over its successive phases and different ages, like veritable seasons of the soul, which, each in their turn, shall produce their respective flowers and fruits.

Youth — Poets have sung youth with the opulence of its gifts, the brilliance of its colors, the outbursts of its strength, the charm of its grace and beauty, and so on.

"Similar to green and leafy forests teased by winds, Youth heaves to every side with the rich dower of life, and some profound murmur continuously prevails throughout its foliage," wrote the poet Maurice de Guérin in his immortal *The centaur*.[61]

Such an image is beautiful. Beautiful especially on account of its veracity and truth.

What characterizes youth is opulence, an overflow of life, the superabundance of things, the impulse towards the future. The devotion, the need to love, to communicate, also characterize this period of life when the soul, newly attached to a body whose elements are new and powerful, feels capable of undertaking a vast career and promises itself long hopes.

Youth is of paramount importance because it is the first leaning toward destiny. In it, forgetfulness of the past is total; the past no longer exists and all its powers are turned toward the future. This is why all moralists and educators have focused their experience and their efforts on this preface to human life, in which the whole book will depend. "The hope of the harvest is in the seed," said German polymath and philosopher Leibniz; meaning that the promise of fruits is equally found in the smile of flowers.

---

61 [Trans. note] M. de Guérin, *The centaur; The bacchante* (Trans. and illus. T. S. Moore. London: Hacon & Ricketts, 1899), pp. 11–12.

Monastic and medieval Christianity completely distorted the notion of life and education. In advocating physical ugliness and contempt for one's body, it failed to understand that the soul shapes its body, as God forms the soul, and that the body must bear the signature of both, which cannot be and must not be other than the signature of Beauty. As long as our century or the centuries that follow do not correct this mistake, we will have done nothing for the true progress of the world. Embellish your bodies if you want to clean up the souls and smooth out the path of destiny. Do not forget, O future educators of human beings, that ugliness is a morbid element.

Therefore we must completely rethink the education of youth, if we wish to accelerate the victories and progress of the coming century. All around it, humans and things, arts, sciences, literature, everything must speak of grandeur, nobility, strength, glory, and beauty.

Whereas the youth of ancient Greece would annually compete in the glorious Olympic festivals, as soon as the youngsters set foot in the famous city, they were seized by the fascinating magic of Beauty. The buildings, with their impeccable symmetry; the Forum, with its superb statues, which sometimes represented the beauty of Hercules and sometimes that of Apollo; the people's religious contest; the majesty of the temples; the harmonious organization of the festival; the wreaths of myrtle and laurel, which already breathed the pride of victory; everything cried out to the young ephebes hastening from the furthest extremities of Attica to fight in the stadium: "O young men, be beautiful, be great, be happy, be strong!" A little farther on, in the sanctuary of Olympia, the sculptor Phidias' Jupiter, radiant with immortal beauty, consecrated, by his divine gesture, this object lesson both solemn and harmonious.

We must resuscitate this discipline of sacred antiquity, if we want to reinvigorate our youth and humanity's strength.

Nowadays everything seems to rest on hard science as a method, and on democracy as a social principle. Nevertheless, these two are under threat. Materialistic science loses its way in dissection and analysis; it breaks down instead of creating, and dissects instead of acting. On the other hand, democracy, in its living works, already bears the seeds of decadence. It advocates mediocrity of all kinds; it outlaws genius and defies force – and the 20th century began powerless and painful on this intellectual and moral premise. The mistake was to take science for an ideal, and democracy for an end, while both are just means to an end and not ends in themselves.

The youth of tomorrow will have to vigorously react against these two idolatries – the youth of today has begun to do it already. There are among our young people some elite spirits, initiates, early warriors who have paved the way and prepared the exodus and the march of the human soul to the future. They are the good Spiritualists, those who know that where the Spirit breathes, there is freedom. This will be the motto of the new legion, that is to say, a free youth, freed from the obstruction of false disciplines; a youth who questions, and also listens to itself; who hears its inner voices and seeks to understand its destiny by studying the mystery and the law of evolution.

It will be the reign of the Spirit, aspired by the souls that love of the heights. True, the goal is far from being achieved yet; it will be necessary to pulverize many idols whose base is rebellious to the demolisher's hammer; nevertheless, everything directs us toward this culmination glimpsed by thinkers, beyond the horizons of our age. A force pushes us there like a sea breeze pushes a skiff; and I hope, before my time of dying, to be able to salute from afar the promised land which the future Sun will illuminate with its morning glory and its brilliant light.

Maturity — Mature age is, in fact, the golden age of life, because it is the time of the harvest, the Messidor[62] where maturation takes place in the heart, in the spirit, in one's whole self. By now, the exuberance of youth will have opened routes like alleys, like clearings that the woodcutter has opened in the opulence of the forest. Illusions, brilliant dreams, will have all but vanished. Underneath the golden mist that once covered things, we now see the sober lines, the austere forms of reality. Those around us no longer have on their forehead the poetic halo that once our creative imagination had put on them. Love itself has revealed to us some of their failings, perhaps even betrayals. Finally, virtue has proved to us that it is sometimes nothing but a word. At this period of life, a great danger threatens most human beings: plain skepticism. Woe to those who let themselves be invaded by this unhealthy worm which neutralizes all the forces of maturity! It is then, on the contrary, that we must recover and awaken in ourselves the holy enthusiasm of youth. Happy are those whose hearts have kept the faith of the early days!

Without a shadow of a doubt, mature age is less poetic, less springlike than adolescence; by now, flowers have fallen taking away their color and their perfume. Yet fruits begin to sprout out from the ends of the soul as from branches of a tree.

In youth, one feels growing up; in the midst of life, one feels mature, and it is one of the most noble and productive stages of human evolution. Mature is, par excellence, the

---

[62] [Trans. note] *Messidor* was the tenth month of the French Republican calendar (introduced in 1793), herein used figuratively as the period of harvesting.

period of fullness; it is the river that flows freely and pours richness and fertility into the meadow.

Among highly evolved souls, rich of accumulated capital from past lives, great works are written or sketched in youth; when their genius is still adolescent, if one can express oneself in this way. Most of the great individuals in history have felt, from their earliest youth, rising on the horizon of their thought, the star which one day was to illuminate their glory and immortality. Christopher Columbus was still a child when visions of the New World haunted him; the great Renaissance painter Raphael had already produced some immortal works before reaching his second youth. Milton was just twelve years old when the first idea of his poem *Paradise Lost* sprang up in his mind. But for the majority of humans – since genius is an exception – talent alone is the ordinary rule. It is in the maturity of life, in the middle of the forest, as expressed by the medieval Italian poet, Dante, that great thoughts as well as great works are accomplished. So, the art of life consists in preparing mature age like a farm laborer prepares the harvest in haste.

It would be necessary to be able to make this medieval period of our existence last a very long time, where the life of the perispirit is in full swing, with all its radiant and vibratory power; and for that, it would be necessary to preserve for as long as possible an essential element of sustenance for action and work: a blood free from impurities, a disciplined nervous system, a vigorous and healthy body. This is the *mens sana in corpore sano* ("a healthy mind in a healthy body") of which spoke the wise minds of antiquity, and which makes reference to a perfect balance of physical, intellectual and moral life.

Then we understand how hard it is to organize and conquer harmony and order in human beings. How many bright and promising young individuals fell off in April like flowers!

The great enemy of mature age, as of one's whole life, is selfishness. Human beings diminish themselves, and are killed by the desire to enjoy. Carnal and cerebral passions burn humans from both ends, so to speak. They empty the marrow of the brain and the heart. The blood does not rejuvenate fast enough to delay old age; and thus, faster than it should, death arrives. We must therefore donate of ourselves so as to be able to recover – self-sacrifice is a preserving element, and those, says the Master, Jesus, who put too much care in guarding their own life, compromise it by the very same reason, and end up losing it. According to Jesus, no one lives as long on Earth as the one who is always ready to die.

"They call you, you flee"; said the poet to death,[63] "I want to live, you come!"

Mature age is the summer of our earthly existence; like the burning season, it is made of ardor, it is full of light. The sunrise is morning; the sunset, is radiant; and the nights, are lit sumptuously by the stars. We feel happy to live, we are aware of its strength and we know how to use it. It is then that the human being physically and morally reaches the culmination of Beauty – for there is beauty in mature age, and it's the real one. It is a mistakes to consider that only the beauty of youth commands life, even if it lacks its main element, which is the force resulting from a general and harmonious balance of the self.

Maturity is the age of victory; though adolescence reveals the rose and the myrtle, it is in mature age that we achieve all life's laurels. Work, inspiration, and love come together to weave us wreaths: this is the solemn hour when the

---

63 [Trans. note] Unnamed in the original, the obscure French poet is Natalie BLANCHET (of St. Gengoux-le-Royal, Burgundy).

trophies are brought to be put at the victorious feet. All the favorable divinities smile and second the individual; vigorous Fortune and the tutelary genius of the nation invite the champion to sacrifice on their altars.[64]

Old age — Old age is the autumn of life; on its last decline, it is winter. Just by uttering this expression – old age – one already feels the cold rising to the heart. Old age, according to common human judgment, is decrepitude and ruin; it is the recapitulation of all sorrows and evils, all life's pains. It is the melancholic and sorrowful prelude to the final goodbye.

Well, this is a serious mistake. First of all, as a general rule, no phase of human life is wholly devoid of gifts of nature, still less so of God's blessings. Why would the last stage of our existence, which immediately precedes the crowning of destiny, be more desolate than the others? This would be a contradiction – and there cannot be any in God's work. Everything is harmony, as in the living composition of an impeccable music concert. Therefore, on the contrary, old age is beautiful, great, and holy; and we are going to study it for a moment, in the pure and serene light of Spiritism.

Roman statesman Cicero wrote an eloquent treatise on old age. No doubt, we find in these famous pages something of the harmonious genius which characterized this great individual. Nevertheless, it is a purely philosophical work which contains only cold views, sterile resignation, and sheer abstractions.

---

[64] [Trans. note] L. DENIS uses ancient Greece's practices and mythology to speak poetically and symbolically of one's mature age.

It is from a different point of view that one must place oneself in order to understand and admire this august peroration of earthly existence.

Old age recapitulates the whole book of life. It summarizes the gifts of other times of one's existence, without any illusions, passions, or errors. The old individual has seen the nothingness of all that was left behind; has glimpsed the certainty of all that will come, and has become a seer. The old individual knows, believes, sees, and waits. Around his or her forehead, crowned with gray hair like the hieratic band worn by ancient pontiffs, the old individual exudes a majesty that is all priestly. In the absence of kings, among certain peoples, it was the Elders who governed.

Old age was, and still is, despite everything, one of the beauties of life, and certainly one of its highest harmonies. It is often said: what a handsome old person! If old age did not have its particular esthetic value, then why this remark?

However, we must not forget that in our time there are, as pointed by François-René de Chateaubriand,[65] a lot of old people but few wise, aged individuals. Indeed, old, wise individuals are kind, indulgent, and love and encourage youth. Their hearts have not aged, whereas those who are merely old people are jealous, malicious and strict; and if our younger generations no longer hold their ancestors in respectful veneration, is it not precisely because the old have lost the high serenity and amiable benevolence so characteristic of the ancient elders? Old age is holy, it is as pure as early childhood; it is through this virtue that it brings us closer to God and that it sees more clearly and further into the depths of the infinite.

---

[65] [Trans. note] F. R. CHATEAUBRIAND wrote "*In our day ... people are old, but they are no longer venerable.*" See Mme SWETCHINE, *The Writings of Madame Swetchine* (Trans. H. W. Preston. Boston: Roberts Brothers, 1869), "On Old Age," III, p. 98.

Actually, it marks the beginning of dematerialization. Insomnia, which is typical of this age, is a material proof of it. Old age seems like a prolonged sleep. It is the eve of eternity, and the old person is like the sentinel advanced on the extreme frontier of life: he or she already has one foot in the promised land and sees the other side, the second side of destiny. Hence these "strange absences," these prolonged distractions, which are taken for a mental weakening, while they are actually only brief explorations in the afterlife, that is to say, phenomena of momentary expatriation. That is what we often fail to understand. Old age, it has often been said, is the evening of life, it is night. True, night of life; yet it displays so many beautiful evenings and sunsets with hints of apotheosis! It is the night – that is still true – but the night is so beautiful with its set of constellations! Like the night, old age has its milky ways, its white and luminous roads, as it should be the splendid reflection of a long lifetime full of virtue, goodness and honor!

Old age is visited by the spirits of the Unseen; it experiences instinctive illuminations; a wonderful gift of divination and prophecy: it can become permanent mediumship and its oracles echo the voice of God. That is why an old person's blessings are twice holy; one must keep in his or her heart the final accents of the old person who dies, as the distant echo of a voice loved by God and respected by fellow humans.

Old age, when dignified and pure, resembles "the ninth book of the sibyl,"[66] which alone is worth the price of all the others, because, by recapitulating them and summing up all human destiny, it cancels the previous volumes.

Let us continue our meditation on old age by studying the inner work that is done in it. "Of all the stories," it has

---

[66] [Trans. note] See Mme SWETCHINE, *The Writings of Madame Swetchine* (Trans. H. W. Preston. Boston: Roberts Brothers, 1869), "On Old Age," III, p. 99.

been said, "the most beautiful is that of souls." And that is true. It is beautiful to penetrate into this inner world and to uncover therein the laws of thought, the secret movements of love.

The soul of the aged, wise person is a mysterious crypt, illuminated by the initial dawn of the sun of the other world. Just as ancient initiations were accomplished in the deep halls of the Pyramids, far from the prying eyes and noises of distracted and unconscious mortals, likewise it is in the underground crypt of one's old age that sacred initiations are accomplished, as a prelude to the revelations of death.

The transformations, or rather the transfigurations, effected in the faculties of the soul by old age, are indeed remarkable. This inner work can be summed up in one word: simplicity. Old age eminently simplifies all things. First it simplifies the material side of life, by suppressing any artificial necessities, those thousand artificial necessities created by our youth and mature age, which complicated our existence turning it into a veritable slavery, a servitude, a tyranny. As I said above, it is when you start spiritualizing through gradual dematerialization.

The same work of simplification is accomplished in one's intellect. Things accepted as facts become more transparent; at the bottom of each word, we find the idea; at the bottom of each idea, we see God.

Old people possess a precious faculty: that of forgetting. All that has been futile and useless in one's life is effaced; you keep in your memory, as in the depths of a crucible, only that which has been truly substantial.

The forehead of an old person has nothing left of the proud and provocative attitude of youth and mature age; instead it leans under the weight of thought like a ripe ear of corn.

The old, wise individual bends his or her head toward their heart. They applies themselves to turning into love all that remains of their faculties, vigor and memories. Old age, then, is not decadence; it is really a progress, a step forward toward an end: as such, it is one of the blessings from Heaven.

Old age is the preface to death; it is what makes it as holy as the solemn vigil of the Initiates of yore, before raising the veil that covered the mysteries. Death is therefore an initiation.

All religions and philosophies have tried to explain death; very few have retained its true character. Christianity has deified it; its saints looked at it nobly in the face, its poets sung it like a deliverance. However, the saints of Catholicism have seen in it only the exoneration of the servitudes of the flesh, the ransom of sin; and for that very reason the funeral rites of Catholic liturgy threw a sort of terror over this peroration, actually so natural, of earthly existence.

Death is simply a second birth; we leave this world in the same way as we entered it, under the rule of the same law.

Some time before death, a silent work is carried out. Dematerialization has already started. Certain signs can be seen, if people surrounding a dying person are not distracted by external things. Disease plays a considerable role here. It completes in a few months, in a few weeks, in a few days perhaps, what the slow work of aging had prepared: it is the work of "dissolution" (departure) of which the Apostle Paul speaks. This word "dissolution" is very significant: it clearly indicates that the organism disintegrates and that the perispirit "unties" itself from the remaining flesh by which it was enveloped.

What is going on at this supreme moment, which all languages call "the agony," that is to say, the last battle? We rush it, we guess it. A great dying poet[67] translated this solemn moment into the following verse:

"Here is the battle between day and night."

Indeed, by then the soul will have entered a twilight state; it is on the extreme limit, at the frontier of two worlds, and is visited by the initial visions of the world it is going to enter. Meanwhile, the world it is leaving behind sends it the ghosts of remembrance, and a whole procession of spirits arrives at the new dawn.

We never die alone, just as we were never born alone. The invisible ones who knew, loved, and assisted us here when we were born, come to help us get rid of the last chains of earthly captivity, in our time of dying.

At this solemn hour, our faculties enlarge, our soul, half cleared, expands; it starts returning to its natural atmosphere, to resume its normal vibrational life; and for this reason some dying persons present some curious phenomena of mediumship. The Bible is full of these supreme revelations. The death of the patriarch Jacob is an accomplished type of dematerialization with its laws. His twelve sons are gathered around his bed, like a living funereal wreath. The old man concentrates in meditation, and after having recapitulated his past, his memories, he prophesies to each of them the future of his family and his race. His sight extends farther still; he sees at the end of time the one who must one day recapitulate all the centuries-long mediumship of ancient Israel: the Messiah – and he shows as the last offspring of his race, the one who will

---

67 [Transl. note] French poet Victor HUGO (1802–1885). Those were his last words. Another contemporary source gives a different version of the verse: *"In me, this is the battle between day and night."*

sum up all the glory of the posterity of Jacob. No Pharaoh, in his pride, died with as much grandeur as this obscure and ignorant old man who was expiring in a corner of the land of Goshen.

Now let us go back to the very act of death. By now, dematerialization has been accomplished, the perispirit emerges from the fleshly envelope, which still lives a few hours, a few days even, of a purely vegetative life. Thus, the successive states of human personality unfold in the reverse order of the one which presided over birth. The vegetative life which had begun in the maternal breast is the last to be extinguished this time, whereas intellectual life and sensory life are the first to depart.

What happens then? The spirit, that is, the soul in its fluidic envelope (the perispirit), and, consequently, the self, carries with it the last moral and physical impression that struck it on Earth; it keeps it for a more or less prolonged time, depending on its degree of evolution. That is why it is important to surround the agony of the dying with sweet and holy words and lofty thoughts, for it is these last noises, these last gestures, these final images that are printed on the pages of the subliminal book of one's consciousness; it is the last line that the dead will read as soon as they enter the afterlife or rather as soon as one becomes aware of one's new mode of being.

Death is, in fact, a passage; it's a transition and a translation. If we were to borrow an image from modern life, I would gladly compare it to a tunnel. Indeed, the soul advances in the procession of death more or less slowly, according to its degree of dematerialization and spirituality.

Higher-order souls, that have always lived in the highest spheres of thought and virtue, traverse this obscurity with the speed of an express train, which comes out in an instant into the full light of the valley. Yet this is the privilege of a small number of evolved spirits: they are the elect and the wise.

I shall not speak here of criminals and animalized beings with gross instincts, that have lived or rather vegetated their entire existence in the lowlands of vice, or in the cesspool of crime. For them, it is dark night, a night full of hideous nightmares. I find it hard, however, to believe that the frontiers of the afterlife and the passage of time while they are in the errant state are peopled by those frightening beings whom Occultists call the elementals. Instead it must be seen only as symbols and images, reflections of passions, vices and crimes that the perverse have committed here below.[68] Let us consider here only the ordinary lives, the average existences which quietly follow the logical phases of their destiny. This is the common condition of most mortals.

Thus the soul enters the dark gallery: it dwells there in the darkness or rather in a darkness close to the light. It is the twilight of the afterlife. Poets have very happily rendered this state and described this half-day, this chiaroscuro of a world out of this world.

At this point, analogies between birth and death are striking. The newborn child remains several weeks in oblivion, before being able to stare at the light and become aware of his or her surroundings. The newborn's eyesight is not yet clear, nor is it clear the radiation that comes from the baby's thoughts.

In the same way, the recently deceased, like a newborn to the invisible world, will also remain oblivious for some time, before becoming aware of this new modality of being and their own destiny. The departed can hear murmurs from afar and near the two worlds; they see movements

---

[68] [Trans. note] *Errant state* (also referred to as *erratic state* or *"erraticity"*) is an old Spiritist terminology with no negative connotations whatsoever, merely referring to any period comprised between reincarnations of a spirit. In English, it literally means *errantry*.

and gestures that they are not able to specify or define. Halfway into the fourth dimension, human individuals lose the precise notion of the third dimension, in which they had hitherto always evolved. They are no longer aware of quantity, number, space, and time, since their senses, which, like so many optical instruments, had helped them to calculate, measure, and weigh, have now been suddenly shut out like a door forever closed. What a strange state in which one's soul has to grope blindly on its path to the Beyond! Yet, such a state is quite real.

At that moment, the magnetic influences of prayer, remembrance, and love can play a considerable role, hastening the advent of revealing clarity which will illuminate this still dormant consciousness, that "lost soul" regarding its destiny. Prayer, in this case, is a true evocation; it is a cry of appeal to the indecisive and wandering soul. This is why the forgetfulness of the dead, the neglect of reverence, are culpable, and deserve similar forgetfulness later on, when our turn comes.

However, this transition period, this halt in the tunnel of death, is absolutely necessary as a preparation for the vision of light that must succeed darkness. It is necessary that our psychical senses gradually become proportionate to the new focus that will enlighten them. An abrupt passage, without any transition, from one life state to another, would be dazzling and produce a long-lasting disturbance. "*Natura non facit saltus*" ("Nature does not make leaps"), said the great Swedish botanist, physician, and zoologist Carl Linnaeus (1707–1778). Well, this law similarly governs the gradual stages of spiritual liberation.

It is necessary that the soul's sense of vision be enlarged, that the night bird, which cannot stare at the rising of the dawn, strengthen its eyesight until it can, like the eagle, look straight into the Sun, with fearless eyes. This preparatory work is gradually accomplished, during the more or less prolonged halt in the tunnel which precedes an errant state[69] life, properly speaking. Little by little, the light is at first very pale like the dawn which rises on the crest of the mountains; then, after dawn comes sunrise; this time, the soul is able to see the new world that it now inhabits: it reads and understands itself, thanks to a subtle light that penetrates thoroughly into its own essence.

Gradually, all your destiny, with your previous lives, and especially with the conscious and reflexive notion of your last incarnation, will be revealed as in a vibrational and animated movie projection. Then the spirit finally understands what it is, where it is, and what it is worth.

Souls go by means of an infallible instinct into a sphere exactly proportional to their degree of evolution, to their ability of enlightenment, to their current aptitude for perfectibility. Fluidic affinities lead them, like a gentle but imperious breeze, which pushes their boat toward other similar souls, with which they will unite in a sort of friendship, of magnetic kinship. And thus life – a truly social life, but of a higher degree – is absolutely restored as formerly here below, for the human soul cannot renounce its nature. The soul's inner structure, its faculty of radiation, will impose on it the society it deserves.

Besides, in the afterlife, families, groups of souls, circles of spirits, are reorganized or reunited according to laws of affinity and sympathy.

Purgatory is visited by angels, mystical theologians used to say. The spiritual plan is visited, directed, and harmonized by higher-order spirits, now say Spiritist thinkers like me.

Here below, among the elect of genius, holiness, and glory, there have been and there always will be initiators. They are predestined, indeed missionaries, who have been

---

[69] [Trans. note] See footnote 69 above.

given the task of advancing the world in truth and justice, at the price of their efforts, their tears, and sometimes their own blood.

Souls' high missions are a constant. The sublime spirits, which have instructed and improved their fellow beings on Earth, continue in a higher world, in a larger setting, their apostolate of light and their redemption through love.

It is thus, as I said at the beginning of these pages, that history eternally recommences and becomes more and more universal. The circular law which presides over the eternal progress of nations and worlds is constantly unfolding in spheres and orbs ever loftier each time; starting all over again in the higher spheres, under the same law that makes everything evolve in the lower-order spheres. The whole secret of the universe lies there.

Souls that are aware of having wasted their last incarnation understand the need to reincarnate and prepare for it. Nothing is stagnant, everything moves in these perpetually vibrating and stirring spheres. It is an incessant, uninterrupted, progressive, and eternal activity.

The work of civilizations on Earth is nothing compared to the harmonious labor of the Unseen. Up there, no material impediment, no fleshly obstacle stops the impetus, discourages or slows growth. No hesitation, no anxiety, no uncertainty. The soul sees the ultimate goal, it knows the means to achieve it, then it rushes itself to achieve it. Who can describe the harmony found in these pure intelligences, the effort of their sturdy willpower, the forceful elan of their love stronger than death?

What language can ever replicate the sublime and fraternal communion of those spirits that hold between them dialogues as ardent as light, as subtle as perfumes, and where each magnetic vibration echoes in the very soul of God? This is the heavenly life; such is eternal life; and it is these perspectives that death opens indefinitely before us! O fellow humans! Understand your destiny, be proud and happy to be alive; do not blaspheme against the law of love and beauty which unfold before your eyes paths that are so wide and radiant! Accept life as it is, with its phases, its alternatives, its vicissitudes; that is only the preface, the prelude to a higher life, where you will soar and hover like the eagle in the immensity of the sky, after having laboriously crawled through a material and imperfect world.

Therefore, it is not by means of a funeral hymn that we must welcome death, but by a song of life; for it is not a cruel evening star that thus rises, but instead, the radiant star of the true morning.

Sing, O soul, the triumphal hymn, the hosanna of the new century, in which all will be born for more glorious destinies. Always ascend higher in the infinite pyramid of light; and as the hero of the legend of Excelsior, pitch your tent on the radiant Mount Tabors[70] of the Incommensurable, of the Eternal!

---

[70] [Trans. note] L. DENIS poetically and symbolically evokes the biblical Mount Tabor, site of the Transfiguration of Jesus.

XVI

MISSION OF THE 20TH CENTURY

When one takes a quick look at history as a whole, which is a veritable book of the destiny of civilizations, it seems that each century has a special role to play, a specific mission to fulfill in the march of humanity.

The 20th century seems to have a vocation superior to that of all others.

In its first half, we are witnessing the collapse of all that was inherited from the past. In its second half, it will lay the foundations of the future world, made of beauty, light, justice, which our contemporaries hail as a distant mirage of this New World of thought and science, which we sense, as Christopher Columbus did in his time, is heading toward unknown territory.

The transition is not without jolts and violent clashes. The spectacle offered by this rumbling decay would be deplorable, were we not sure that great ruins are followed by great resurrections.

History, indeed, only erases to write again; thought demolishes only to rebuild: it is the evolution law, the logical progress of humanity.

We are witnessing the collapse of all religions, or rather rituals and forms of worship; for religion in its principle, in its essence – that is to say, as the impulse of the soul toward the infinite, as the aspiration of all intelligences toward the divine ideal – religion is as indestructible as truth, as inexhaustible as love, and as unalterable as beauty.

What must perish and are likely to disappear entirely are the old dogmatic formulas and self-righteous hypocrisy, along with the obsolete disciplines of organized religion; also, the whole priestly apparatus and the worship of idols.

The Catholic religion in particular has collapsed under the weight of its centuries-old faults.

The Roman Church has long been a political power. Its pontiffs misunderstood their mission, its priests lost the sense of the deep and sacred initiation of the First Christians.

Thus, the rupture between the Church and modern society, this split between the spirit of Rome and that of the century, was accentuated by the abolition of the Concordat and by the attitude of the pope during the last war.[71]

We are also witnessing the collapse of science, not true science as claimed by the scholar Ferdinand Brunetière, because it cannot perish – true science never tires in its investigations – but materialistic science, the one that dominated the world for over a hundred years.

In the late 19th century, French writer and researcher Ernest Renan published a book on *The Future of Science* (Boston, Roberts Brothers, 1891), a cleverly crafted book that enjoyed a certain popularity. He prophesied the disappearance, in a short time, of the concept of mystery, which, in various forms, poses as a challenge to human thought.

---

[71] [Trans. note] *Concordat* was an agreement between the Vatican and a secular government relating to matters of mutual interest. In context, "last war" refers specifically to World War I (1914–1918).

Well, not only has mystery subsisted but even multiplied, thanks to the discovery of radioactivity and the development of psychical phenomena.

Other examples will show to what extent official science, while proclaiming its victories over matter, has been powerless to solve the great mysteries which concern the human soul and its faculties.

In his book *The Riddle of the Universe*, German polymath Ernst Haeckel (1834–1919) wrote something like: "As long as the riddle of substance, which recapitulates all other riddles, is not solved, nothing will have been done to the satisfaction of the human spirit."[72]

Henri Poincaré, one of the masters of modern science, struck with death in the midst of his labors, showed in one of his last books that science is still a hypothesis. He also confessed that *all laws of physics are to be revised.*

Physicist, physiologist and physician Arsène d'Arsonval used much the same language in his lectures at the Collège de France.

Now let us see what American philosopher and psychologist William James, professor of philosophy at Harvard University, wrote on the same subject in the last pages of his fine book, *The Varieties of Religious Experience*. He declares that every time he puts himself into a sectarian scientist's attitude, imagining that the world of sensations and matter is all there is, he immediately hears the warnings of an "inward monitor." A few lines further, he adds:[73]

"The total expression of human experience, as I view it objectively, invincibly urges me beyond the narrow 'scientific' bounds. Assuredly, the real world is of a

---

[72] [Trans. note] *Cf.* L. DENIS's short paraphrase above with E. HAECKEL, *The Riddle of the Universe* (Trans. J. McCabe. London: Watts & Co., 1934), *passim* and "Conclusion."

[73] [Trans. note] W. JAMES, *The Varieties of Religious Experience* (London and Bombay: Longmans, Green & Co., 1902), p. 519.

different temperament – more intricately built than physical science allows."

It is precisely this real world, the psychical world, that most of our scientists do not want to know; instead of studying, as they should, life in its higher manifestations, they lose themselves in infinitesimal analysis. They see, so to speak, only the dust of things and ideas.

Official science has always lacked independence and freedom. At first, it went astray by slavishly submitting itself to the authority of the Church; then, by becoming subservient to the materialistic doctrines of the 18th century, and soon thereafter, to Germanic pantheism. Finally, for almost a century, it has become a satellite of positivism, this incomplete philosophical system, which is systematically losing interest in the greatest problem that the human spirit wants to and must resolve, namely, that of its own origin and destiny. Instead, it confines itself to dragging along the world its dry and banal formulas, like a "Wingless Victory,"[74] which, exactly for lacking wings, was condemned to crawl without ever being able to ascend toward the summits.

Skeptical science had put the law of numbers at the base of everything. From then on, life has become a kind of algebra whose equations led us to one or more unknown forces. Such an orientation goes in the opposite direction of Nature; for humans exist to create and not to decompose; to act and not just to analyze. This negative system has rendered the labors of our scientists sterile; and it is thus that for a long time we have seen the human character and conscience, the arts, ideals, and beauty, all gradually subside before our eyes.

---

[74] [Trans. note] In ancient Greece, Nike was originally the "winged victory" goddess. The absence of wings in the Athena Nike led Athenians to call it *Apteros Nike* ("wingless victory"); later on, a story emerged that the statue was devoid of wings so that it could never fly away.

In fact, science has disregarded the law of aesthetics by consecrating a naturalism that dissects life, instead of developing it. In morality, it advocated determinism, which posits in principle the powerlessness of effort and the renunciation of action. In the social order, it put forward that an endless crumbling of powers and responsibilities at times produces a state of affairs that verges on disorder and confusion.

Science had the mission of building society on new foundations; instead, it destroyed without having built anything. By losing sight of the great summits, the great sources of thought, skeptical science has cooled the human heart. It destroyed the high ideal that brings poetry to life and makes it bearable. That is why the rising generations seem disillusioned and clamor for something else.

The problem of politics is no less serious. Under the pressure of events, most of the monarchical institutions have collapsed, and triumphant democracy flourishes over their ruins, but within them an intense crisis has been raging. The elements of anarchy grow and spread. The fates of materialistic science and that of present-day socialism are correlated; they are inspired by the same methods and formulas.

It must be admitted that socialist democracy today is in disagreement with the very principle of the French Revolution. This latter was essentially individualistic; it wanted to give everyone free initiative in their personal actions. The current regime acts differently: it tends to level down all strong individualities and to logically pass from an equality of rights to a de facto equality. It goes to collectivism, that is, to the negation of the human person and its absorption into the social whole. It is not through statism that we would be rid of mediocrity; on the contrary, it would be by nature its protector. Nor is it the regulation of work by the collectivity that will give the proletariat the happiness that the utopians of the day dangle before their eyes.

All human beings are equal, some say. In its narrow historical sense, that formula may seem accurate; but there can be no question here of a real, absolute equality. If humans are equal in rights, they will always be unequal in intelligence, in faculties, in morality. To say otherwise would be to deny the law of evolution, which obviously does not act with the same efficiency upon all individuals.

A free man on a free soil! This will be the social ideal of the future. But it is necessary to take into account the necessity of Loving Fellowship as a prerequisite, which alone, through harmony, can balance freedom.

Centuries have fled since the heroic age of the First Christians, where they sold whatever they possessed so that the apostles would distribute the money thus obtained among all, according to the needs of each person. This principle of true loving fellowship, of which the protagonists of the French Revolution were reminded by Gabriel Bonnot de Mably, apparently is nowhere to be found today. It is certainly not in current social habits and practices which reflect only selfishness. Instead, it can be detected in the aspirations of the human soul, in this movement which agitates crowds from one end of the Earth to the other: it lies in distant, future ages!

~

After reviewing the ruins that the 20th century has already seen happen, I will now talk about the renovations being prepared by it, and which will certainly be achieved.

It is always in the intellectual realm that big innovations start. Ideas precede and prepare facts. This is the logic of history and the law of human progress.

Excessive use of analytical methods and procedures has nearly lost us the day. Instead, major syntheses and overall conceptions are the ones that should necessarily be devised. Behold, there is a new point of view on all things. In order to apply new methods, new minds are required. The free science of tomorrow requires free spirits.

As long as individuals of this generation, subject to the disciplines of the Church or the University, do not disappear, we can only sketch a work of redemption of the human spirit. The Church with its confessions, the University with its examinations, have distorted the springs of the soul and oppressed the impulsions of thought. Hearts and intellects have withdrawn into themselves; no one had the time or space to feel and live fully. Nevertheless, a work of innovation is being prepared. The 19th century and the beginning of the 20th century have seen its forerunners emerge. Human geniuses will not be long in coming.

In each period of history, there are a certain number of spirits who belonged rather to the next century than to the century in which they lived and, for that very reason, resemble superior beings out of place, strange individuals utterly disturbing to their contemporaries.

Shakespeare once wrote that, "Coming events cast their shadows before them," before their presence shakes the universe.

Indeed, forerunners have seen this magnificent shadow appear in their path, wearing moving and powerful forms. They have sensed things and guessed the laws. This is the sign of their intellectual excellence and their vocation; yet this is also the reason for their isolation, their abandonment, their suffering in the midst of the crowd that is unable to understand them.

Events have arisen in their tragic grandeur. For over four years, nations have come up against tremendous shocks. The war continued its work of ruin and death, but at the same time it swept away many errors, delusions and fantasies. Under the breath of the storm, clouds were torn apart, and a corner of blue sky appeared.

The 19th century was the century of matter; the 20th will be the century of the spirit. The former, by scrutinizing nature, has brought forth unknown energies; whereas the 20th century will reveal spiritual forces, superior to all that we humans have dreamed, and the study of these forces will lead us to solving the problem of life and death. Forerunners have been great before History! They are the ones who illuminate the march of humanity on the long road of destiny. They are like the runners at the ancient stadium, of whom Lucretia speaks, who pass from hand to hand the sacred torch of inspiration. Without them, the intellectual innovations of the world would find neither open paths nor well-prepared spirits. Among these, one can cite Allan Kardec, Jean Reynaud, Flammarion, Victor Hugo, William Crookes, F. W. H. Myers, Oliver Lodge, and many others.

Myers' book *Human Personality* (London, 1903) ends with a fine spiritualistic synthesis. The author demonstrates that we must first explain humans to humans themselves. Learning to know the human being, he says, leads to the knowledge of God and the universe. This was already recommended by the British poet Alexander Pope (1688–1744) in *An Essay on Man*.

Yet, generations go by and this essential study of the inner self is always neglected.

The 19th century has devoted incalculable resources and immense labors to the study of the material universe. It prodigiously extended the field of its observations and experiments; however the world still does not know the inner constitution of the human being and the laws of human destiny.

As a result, our legislators are unable to govern. How, indeed, to direct people, to administer a nation, when one ignores, or pretends to ignore the great principle of life! From whence came out the malaise that afflicts our country today.

The formidable problem of work for all citizens, with its many difficulties, has no other origin than this capital error. We have wished to see in the human person only a body to be nourished and exploited, and from there we have become concerned only with a person's material needs. The struggle for life has become as brutal as it was in barbaric times.

The damage is great and it is not with empirical systems that it will be cured. It will be neither in socialism in its present form nor in collectivism, that remedies will be found.

We must first search for the causes and tackle them. Now, these are, so to speak, an integral part of humans. It is human errors that must be corrected, human passions that must be fought, by acting less on the mass and more on the individual. It is the individual who must be enlightened and amended; we must cultivate and develop the inner self in each living personality, if we want to move from a reign of matter to a reign of the spirit.

For a new science, we need individuals who know thoroughly the higher laws of the universe, the principle of immortal life, and the great law of evolution – which is a law of love and not an "iron law," as proposed by Haeckel.

There is a philosophy at once as old as the world, and young as the future because it is eternal, being the truth; a philosophy which summarizes all the fundamental notions of life and destiny: *Spiritism*, of which the book of F. W. H. Myers, cited above, is only a scientific commentary.

Spiritism has burst into the world; it is overflowing on all sides. What can learned society, weekly magazines, or daily newspapers (only interested in its phenomena and manifestations) do to deny, criticize, distort or combat it?

Spiritism is the issue of the moment, the universal problem. It is no longer possible to remain indifferent to it!

And it is precisely because this spiritual invasion fills the two worlds and occupies human thought, that I have felt obliged to insist on the duties incumbent on me with reference to this new faith, this young and strong science which offers irrefutable proofs of life after death, containing in germ all the resurrections of the future!

Finally, let us recall the essential character of Modern Spiritualism (i.e., Spiritism). It is not a new system to be added to other systems, nor a set of vain theories. It is a solemn act in the drama of human evolution that begins, a revelation that illuminates both the depths of the past and those of the future, bringing out of the dust of centuries dormant beliefs, to animate them with a new flame which revive them in order to complete them.

It is a powerful breath that descends from the spiritual world and spreads all over the world. Under its action all the great truths awake. Majestic, they emerge from the dark ages to play the role that divine thought has assigned them. Great things are fortified in contemplation and silence. In the apparent oblivion of the centuries, they draw new energies. They retreat in themselves and get ready for future tasks.

Above the ruins of temples, extinguished civilizations and collapsed empires; above the ebb and flow of human tides; a powerful voice rises, exclaiming: *The time has come, the time has arrived!*

From the starry depths, spirits descend in legions on Earth, to fight the fight of light against darkness. It is no longer humans, it is no longer the wise and philosophers who bring the new tenets. It is the geniuses of the spiritual world that come among us and breathe in our thought the teachings called to regenerate the world. They are the spirits of God! All those who possess the gift of spirit sight can see them hovering above us, mingling with our labors, fighting beside us for the redemption and ascension of the human soul.

Great things are about to happen. May the workers of thought rise up, if they want to participate in the mission offered by God to all who love and serve Truth.

SUPPLEMENTAL NOTES

No. 1

ON THE NEED FOR AN INITIAL MOTOR
TO EXPLAIN PLANETARY MOTIONS

→ On this subject, Professor Jean Bulliot wrote in the French journal *Revue du Bien*:

"Obviously, said Aristotle, all beings that make up nature are a priori divided into three categories: those that receive movement without giving it; those that receive it and transmit it to other bodies, remaining mere agents of transmission; and finally, the primary sources of movement, which give it fullness without receiving anything from without. The necessity of seeking outside the bodies for the primary source of the movements that animate them is evident in the strictly mechanical hypothesis of Descartes, according to which bodies devoid of all activity remain absolutely passive, given the fact that they receive impulses from without. But, whatever the hypothesis we may come out with about the inner nature of matter, it suffices, in order to justify the necessity of resorting to a primary motor, to encounter in bodies a movement or a class of movements which cannot be explained by ordinary forces."

"Now, this class of movements is found in the revolutions of planets, which revolve around the Sun, the center of the system. This movement of translation, almost circular or elliptical, is due to two concurrent forces: a force of gravitation, which tends constantly to bring the planets down to the Sun, depending on the vertical; and a centrifugal force, which tends to throw them off in a straight line, following the orbital tangent. Now, where does this centrifugal force come from? Only from a primeval impetus by a extraneous cause, given once for all to a planet, at the origin of its revolutions. This impetus is in every respect analogous to that which a child communicates to a stone by making it turn quickly with the help of a slingshot. No natural force can explain this. So Newton does not hesitate to make this great remark at the end of his *Philosophiæ Naturalis Principia Mathematica* [*Mathematical Principles of Natural Philosophy*]: 'The world cannot be explained by the laws of mechanics.' In an enthusiastic drive, his great soul rushes to God, which alone with Its mighty hand, has been able to launch the worlds on the tangents of their orbits. Never have human science, never have human genius, risen higher than in this celebrated page, worthy of crowning Newton's magnificent book."

"With Kant and Laplace, astronomy took another step forward. It establishes the hypothesis of a vast nebula animated by a powerful movement of rotation on itself. As a result of this movement, the planets are detached one by one, as of themselves, from a common mass, whose central core would finally give birth to the Sun. From then on, it seems that everything was changed and that the idea of God became foreign to astronomy. Laplace does not mention God's name even once. But from the strict viewpoint of an explanation of facts, is this silence justified? No way. The question remained for us exactly how it was for Newton. As before, after the hypothesis of the nebula, the problem remains the same. If nothing counterbalanced gravity, always present and always active, then planets would fall and rush straight into the sun. Or rather, nothing would exist to detach them from the common nebula. The latter's gyratory movement alone could provide the necessary centrifugal force. And then again, and in the same terms, there is the great unavoidable problem that we tried in vain to pass over in silence: where does the gyratory movement balance with gravity?"

"Only Kant dared to answer how gravity and repulsive forces are developed by interatomic shocks. Kant was not a mathematician, and it shows all too well here. By virtue of the principle of equality of action and reaction, the molecules, after the shock, develop the same force in one direction as in the opposite direction, from left to right same as from right to left. They are unable, therefore, to generate in the nebula the slightest overall rotation."

"Motionless at first, the nebula would remain forever motionless and, for lack of strength, planets would never form. If, in fact, they had detached themselves from the central mass, it was because the latter turned on itself, and if it turned, it was because the same creative power that Newton had ostensibly invoked, had imparted this movement while forming the nebula."

"When interviewed, Misters Wolf and Puiseux, astronomers of the Observatoire de Paris, had no difficulty in acknowledging it: 'The hypothesis proposed by Kant,' concludes Puiseux, 'must be regarded as inoperative.' 'You need an initial motor,' writes Wolf." (The same opinion is also expressed by C. Flammarion in his books.)

"As for Laplace, basically, implicitly, he may not have said anything different because, if he does not name God literally, he speaks of a nebula in a state of gyration and, on several occasions, he wrote that, in its overall movement, the sum of the areas described by its molecules around the axis is necessarily zero. So, like Newton, he also admitted to be incapable of explaining the movements of the solar system by mere laws of mechanics."

No. 2
OF UNKNOWN FORCES

→ The following is what Mr. G. Lebon said about this important subject:

"Going back to the causes of emission of emanations which can be released from all the bodies with vertiginous speed, we would notice the existence of an intra-atomic energy, unknown until now, and which exceeds all the forces known by its colossal magnitude. We know how to liberate it only in a relatively small quantity, but from the calculation of this quantity it can be deduced that, if it were possible to release entirely all the energy contained in one gram of any type of matter, it could produce a reaction equal to that achieved by the burning of several million tons of coal. In my view, matter appears to be a huge reservoir of energy."

(*Revue Scientifique*, Paris, France, October 17, 1903)

No. 3
CELESTIAL WONDERS; MAGNITUDES AND MASSES OF STARS

→ The magnitudes of some stars are truly formidable. Our Sun is, as we know, 1,300,000 times larger than the Earth, but Sirius exceeds it twelve times in size, and Procyon sixteen times. Deneb in the constellation of Cygnus; the second star of the Great Bear (Ursa Major); Vega, the beautiful blue star of the constellation of Lyra; and Pollux in the constellation of Gemini, are also majestic stars, giant lighthouses scattered in the sidereal night, near which our Sun would be like a mere bright spot. Then there is Capella, a gigantic star, 5,800 times bigger than our Sun; and Arcturus which, in spite of its fearful distance, still shines with a glow that eclipses all the stars in our northern sky. Lastly, there is Betelgeuse in the constellation of Orion.

This time, not even the most prodigious imagination can find words to express this frightening vision. These two stars, Arcturus and Betelgeuse, are each worth several thousand suns like ours. Between them and our solar star, there is almost the same proportion as between our Sun and the Earth.

And yet, astronomy has found an even greater star that eclipse all the others. In order to see it, you have to go to the southern regions, where it shines in the constellation Carina; it is Canopus, the brightest star[75] known to date, for it equals 8,760 suns together.

Of all the stars studied through the telescope, whose distance, light, heat and movement were attempted to be measured, Canopus has been the subject of a special study by British astronomer Oliver Rowland Walkey,[76] a member of the Royal Astronomical Society of London. His study seems to indicate that this prodigious star may be the center of our universe.

The distance from Canopus would be about 489 light years,[77] that is to say, a ray of light arriving from this star today must have been originated in the 16th century AD.

However, his formidable star is not the pivot around which our Sun moves. It is around Alcyone, a star of the Pleiads cluster, located in the shoulder of the constellation Taurus, around which our solar system completes one of its major revolutions in twenty-two and a half million years. A ray of light coming from Alcyone has to travel 715 years before it can reach Earth. There are

---

[75] [Trans. note] Despite L. Denis's statement, astronomers consider Sirius to be the brightest star in the night sky.

[76] [Trans. note] See O. R. Walkey, various articles published in scientific magazines such as *Nature* and *Scientific American*, in the summer of 1916.

[77] [Trans. note] Nowadays astronomers have updated and calculated that distance as being 309.8 light years.

stars whose light does not reach us until 5,500 years
have passed.

The cluster of Pleiads consists of a thousand stars, of
which only seven are visible to the naked eye. Alcyone
is only of the 3rd magnitude, but these main stars are
animated by a uniform and parallel movement, which is
remarkable and also explains why their attraction is even
more powerful than that of the gigantic Canopus.

No. 4
ABOUT THE MUSIC OF THE SPHERES [78]

→ "The solar vibration," says Azbel (*Harmonie des
Mondes*, Paris, 1903, p. 22), "projects through space the
spherical sweeping of the harmonics of its fundamentals,
not only in the apparent form of invisible planets, but in
principle and essentially under the ethereal expression of
harmonic waves, according to a regular progression 1,
2, 3, 4, 5, 6, 7, 8, 9, 10, etc. It is by the direct currents of
these waves that planetary bodies move directly, and by
the circular currents – resembling wave sines formed at the
nodes of confluence of successive, composite waves – that
these planetary bodies are at the same time complexly
geared around the master vibration."

"However, planetary bodies are subject to a large variety
of their particular esthetics of volume, mass or density, in
addition to those of their elliptic revolutions, etc., which
combine to modify more or less their theoretical itineraries.
Whence some substantial aerial evolutions that at first seem
to be deviations. Yet their esthetic computation makes it

---

[78] [Trans. note] All editions of this book's original, published during
L. DENIS's lifetime, list *only* supplemental notes **No. 1, No. 2** and **No. 3.**
Though collected from his other writings, the remaining notes, namely,
Nos. 4, 5, 6 and 7, were later added after his death, by an anonymous hand.

possible for one to perceive their harmonic character, side by side with their simple mathematical character."

No. 5
ABOUT EXPERIMENTAL SPIRITUALISM OR SPIRITISM

→ Now more than ever, Spiritism has drawn all sorts of public attention. There is often some talk of haunted houses, occult phenomena, apparitions, spirits' materializations. Science, literature, the theater and the press are intertwined with these and the experiments of the Society of Psychical Research, the revelations of the great British publisher William Thomas Stead, the testimony of Prof. William James. Investigations carried out by some Paris newspapers constantly render the subject with updated relevance.

Let us examine this issue, inquiring why Spiritism, so often buried, reappears incessantly, and has rapidly increased the number of its adherents every day.

Is it not strange? Perhaps never in history has anything similar happened before. Never have we seen a set of facts, considered at first to be impossible – the mere idea of which raised only aversion, suspicion and disdain in the minds of most people, and the hostility of many age-old institutions – end up drawing so much attention and even the conversion of educated and capable individuals, as accredited by their functions and their character. And such individuals, initially skeptical, came to study, research, experiment, acknowledge and affirm the reality of these phenomena.

The celebrated British chemist and physicist William Crookes, known all over the world for his discovery of radiant matter; and who, for three years, obtained in private seances materializations of the Spirit Katie King, under rigorous control conditions; speaking of these manifestations

198 THE BIG ENIGMA

once said: "I do not say that it is possible; I say that it actually is so."

Oliver Lodge, rector of the University of Birmingham and member of the Royal Academy of Sciences, wrote: "I am, for all personal purposes, convinced of the persistence of human existence beyond bodily death; ... it is a belief which has been produced by scientific evidence."

In his fine book *Human Personality* (London,1903), F. W. H. Myers, a lecturer at Cambridge, whom the 4th International Congress of Psychology, Paris, 1900, had elected honorary president, arrives at the conclusion that voices and messages are coming back from beyond the grave. Speaking of the medium Mrs. Thompson, he writes[79] (paraphrased): "I believe that most of these messages come from spirits that are temporarily using the mediums' body to convey them to us."

Famous Professor Lombroso, of Turin (Italy), declared in the periodical *La Lettura*: "The cases of haunted houses in which for years apparitions and noises made themselves manifest as a sequence to tragic deaths – facts which are independent of the presence of mediums – argue in favor of the intervention of the dead. There are many cases where such phenomena have been known to extend over several generations and even over several centuries."[80]

Well-known philosopher Émile Boutroux, in brilliant lectures, talks about spirits and mediumistic communications, and assures that "The subliminal door is the opening through which the divine can enter the human

[79] For MYERS's original text, see *Proceedings of the SPR*, vol. XVII (1901-1903), pp. 67–74.

[80] [Trans. note] Extracted from L. DENIS, *Joan of Arc* (Trans. A. C. Doyle. London: John Murray, 1924), paraphrased and adapted by L. Denis from the French counterpart of the *Annals of Psychical Science*, London, April 1908.

soul." "Sometimes," he says, "spiritualistic revelations are so strange that it seems that the subject [the medium] is in communication with beings other than those normally available to him or her."[81]

William James, professor of philosophy at Harvard University, New York, the eminent psychologist who, until his death, asserted the plausibility of communications from the dead, published in 1909 in the *Proceedings of the SPR*, a study about his deceased friend, Hodgson, who came to talk to him through the medium Mrs. Piper. He wrote that "Such expressions and phrases were quaintly characteristic of R[ichard] H[odgson] in the body, and as they appear, often rapidly and spontaneously, they give the almost irresistible impression that it is really the Hodgson personality, presiding with its own characteristics."[82]

It is in America that we find the original home of Spiritism, or Modern Spiritualism. In reality, beyond-the-grave phenomena are encountered at the basis of all great religions and philosophies of the past. In almost all eras, relationships have bonded the unseen world with the world of the living. However, in India, Egypt and Greece, this study was the exclusive privilege of a small number of researchers and initiates, who kept the results carefully hidden.

To make such a study possible for all, to make known the real laws that govern the unseen world, to teach humans to see inside these phenomena, as no longer a supernatural order of things, but instead as a hitherto ignored domain of Nature and life, it was required the immense labor of centuries past, all the discoveries of science, all the conquests of the human spirit over matter. It was necessary that human beings became aware of their true place in the

---

[81] *Annales des Sciences Psychiques*, Paris, June 1–16, 1910.

[82] [Trans. note] *Proceedings of the SPR* (Glasgow, 1909), vol. XXIII, part LVIII, p. 37.

universe, that we should learn to measure the weakness of our senses, their impotence to explore by themselves and without help all the domains of living Nature.

Science, by means of inventions, has attenuated this limitation of our organs. The telescope has opened to our eyes the abysses of deep space; the microscope revealed to us things infinitely small. Life has appeared to us everywhere, in the world of the single-celled organisms as well as on the surface of the orbs, giants which roll in the depths of the heavens. Physics has discovered the laws that regulate the transformation of forces, the conservation of energy, and those that maintain balance among worlds. The radioactivity of bodies has revealed the existence of unknown and incalculable powers: X-rays, radio waves, radiations of all kinds and degrees. Chemistry has made us aware of the combinations of substances. Steam and electricity have come to revolutionize the face of the Earth, facilitating international relations and the manifestations of thought, so that an idea can radiate and be propagated from all points of the earthly sphere.

Today the study of the invisible world completes this magnificent ascension of thought and science. The problem of the hereafter stands before the human spirit with power and authority.

Towards the end of the 19th century, we humans, disappointed by all the contradictory theories, by all the incomplete systems which we were intended to feed our thought, letting ourselves slide downhill to doubt, and causing us to lose more and more the notion of future life. It was then that the invisible world came to us and sought us even in our homes. By various means, the dead have manifested themselves to the living. The voices from beyond the grave have spoken. After a long silence, the mysteries of ancient Eastern sanctuaries, the occult phenomena of the Middle Ages, have all been renewed; and Spiritism was born.

It is beyond the seas, in a new world rich in vital energy and ardent expansion, less jaded, dulled by routine than old Europe – and less filled with prejudices of the past – that the first manifestations of Modern Spiritualism were produced. From there they have spread all over the globe. This choice was profoundly wise. Free America was the most favorable environment for the work of diffusion and renovation. Today there are twenty million "modern spiritualists" in America.

But on both sides of the Atlantic, although with different intensities, the phases of progression of the concept of the spirit were the same.

Previously, on both continents, the study of magnetism and fluids had prepared some souls for the observation of the invisible world.

In the beginning, strange facts occurred everywhere, facts of which one dared not speak except in a low voice, in confidence. Then, little by little, the tone rose. Prominent people and scholars, whose names alone would serve to recommend their honor and integrity, have ventured to speak aloud of these facts and attest to them. There was talk of hypnotism, of suggestion; then came telepathy, the cases of levitation, and all the phenomena of Spiritism.

Mediumistic tables started to turn in crazy circles; objects moved without contact; raps were heard in the walls and furniture. A whole set of phenomena was taking place, manifestations which were apparently crude, but perfectly adapted to the requirements of the earthly environment, and to the materialistic and skeptical state of mind of modern society.

These phenomena spoke to the senses, for the senses are like openings through which a fact can penetrate into our understanding. Impressions produced on the body arouse surprise, induce research, and may lead one to be convinced. Hence this chain of events, this ascending progression of phenomena.

Indeed, after a first physical and rough phase, the man-ifestations took on a new aspect. Raps developed regular rhythmic intervals until they became an intelligent and conscious mode of communication; automatic writing also began to propagate. The possibility of contacts between the visible world and the invisible world emerged as a large-scale fact, upsetting conventional wisdom, shaking customary teachings, but opening a path to future life that humans still hesitated to cross, dazzled as we were by the vast perspectives that opened before us.

At the same time that it spread, Spiritism was met with much opposition and hostility against it. Like all new ideas, Spiritism had to contend with contempt, slander, and moral persecution. And like the early Christian idea, it was overwhelmed with bitterness and insults. It is always like that. Whenever new aspects of Truth are revealed to humans, there is always astonishment, distrust and hostility in reaction to them.

This is easily understandable. Humanity has exhausted the old forms of thought and belief, and when unexpected forms of truth are revealed, they seem to respond very little to the ancient ideal which has weakened but not died. Thus a long period of examination, reflection, and incubation is necessary for a new idea to find its way into public opinion. Hence the struggles, the uncertainties, the distresses of the first hour.

The forms of New Spiritualism have been much mocked. The unseen powers that watch over humanity are bet-ter judges than we are of which means should be em-ployed act upon and train us, according to time and place, in order to bring human beings back to the feeling of their role and destinies, without ever hindering our free will. For an essential reason: human freedom must remain untouched.

A higher willpower always knows how to adapt new forms of the eternal revelation to the needs of a specific epoch or civilization. Such revelation gives rise to thinkers, experimenters and scientists in societies, who will point the way and prepare the ground. Their work unfolds itself slowly. Results are weak and imperceptible at first, but the idea gradually penetrates thinking minds. This movement, for being unnoticed, is sometimes only safer and deeper for that very reason.

In this day and age, science has become the sovereign master, the ruler of any intellectual movement. Tired of metaphysical speculations and religious dogmas, humanity demanded sensible proofs, solid foundations on which to base its convictions. It has clung itself to experimental research and close observation of facts as a plank of salvation. Hence the great credit given today to scientists. This is why revelation has taken on a scientific tone. It is through material facts that one manages to draw human attention, for humans have become materialistic themselves.

Mysterious phenomena found scattered throughout the history of the past have happened again and again, and multiplied around us. They have succeeded one another in a progressive order, which seems to indicate a preconceived plan, the execution of a thought, of a will.

In fact, as New Spiritualism has gained ground, phenomena were transformed. The coarse manifestations of the beginning became more refined, took on a higher profile. Mediums received, through writing in a mechanical or intuitive way, messages, inspirations from extraneous sources. Musical instruments could be heard playing by themselves. Voices and songs were also heard; penetrating melodies seemed to descend from the sky and astonish the most incredulous. Direct writing occurred inside juxtaposed and sealed slates. Phenomena of "incorporation" (psychophony) allowed the deceased to take possession of the body of a sleeping subject (a medium), and to talk to those who had known them on Earth. Gradually, and as a result of a planned development, writing mediums, speaking mediums, and healers began to appear everywhere.

Finally, the inhabitants of the spiritual plane, clad in temporary envelopes, have come to mingle with humans, living for a moment in their material earthly life, allowing to be seen, touched, and photographed; and leaving casting molds of their hands and faces momentarily materialized, then vanishing again to resume their ethereal life in the spirit world.

It was thus that, for at least half-century before the writing of this book, a whole chain of events took place, from the most inferior and coarse to the most subtle, depending on the degree of elevation of the intelligences which intervened; all sorts of manifestations occurred under the watchful eyes of researchers and observers.

Also, despite the difficulties involved in experimentation, and regardless of cases of imposture and other modes of exploitation which sometimes surrounded such phenomena, the prejudice, apprehension and distrust were gradually attenuated as the number of serious examiners increased exponentially.

For fifty years in all countries, Spiritist phenomena have been the subject of frequent inquiries, undertaken and directed by scientific commissions. Skeptical scholars, famous professors from all the greatest universities in the world, have subjected these facts to a rigorous in-depth examination. At first, their intention was to shed some light on what they thought was the result of deceit or hallucinations. But almost all of them, however incredulous, and after years of conscientious studies and persistent experimentation, have abandoned their prejudices and bowed to the reality of the facts.

Spiritual manifestations, witnessed by thousands of people in every corner of the world, have shown that an invisible world is stirring around us, or on the spiritual plane. A world where, in a fluidic, etherized state, live all those who have preceded us on Earth, where they have struggled and suffered, and also constitute beyond death a second humanity.

New Spiritualism (Spiritism) surrounds itself today with a parade of evidence and a large group of testimonies, so imposing that doubt is no longer possible for researchers in good faith. This is what Professor Challis of Cambridge University (UK) wrote on the subject:

"The testimony has been so abundant and consentaneous that either the facts must be admitted to be such as are reported, or the possibility of certifying facts by human testimony must be given up."[83]

Also, the movement of dissemination of Spiritism has increased more and more. Currently we are witnessing a real flourishing of the Spiritist idea. Belief in the invisible world has spread throughout the face of the Earth. Spiritism has experimental societies and groups in many countries, with facilitators, journals and newspapers.

Would that philosophy, in its boldest speculations, could have raised itself to the conception of another mode of existence after the death of one's fleshly body! Alas, human science has not yet been able to assert through experiments the truth of the fact itself. Thus the merit of Spiritism is to provide us with such experiments, by proving the possibility of communication, under certain conditions, of the living with intelligences that have lived among us before passing into the realm of invisible life. In some cases, these

---

[83] [Trans. note] See *The Spiritual Magazine*, vol. VI, p. 422, James Burns, London, 1871. Later quoted in A. Russel WALLACE, *Miracles and Modern Spiritualism* (rev. ed., London: George Redway, 1896), p. 101.

souls have been able to furnish proofs of identity and state of consciousness.

To cite only one example, Australian-born psychical researcher Dr. Richard Hodgson, who died in December 1905, had since communicated with his friend James Hyslop, a professor at Columbia University, entering into minute details about the experiments and the work developed by the Society for Psychical Research (SPR), of which he was president for the American branch. He explained how these experiments should be conducted, and by doing so he absolutely proved his identity.

These communications are transmitted through different mediums, who do not know each other; and they are confirmed by one another. Words and phrases frequently used by the spirit communicator during his life on Earth are immediately recognizable.

~

Regardless of the fact that Spiritism faced difficult beginning, and its progress was relatively slow, forced to contend with all sorts of obstacles, after ten years it became legitimately established. Spiritism has become a real science as well as a philosophical system and a school of thought. It offers a general philosophy of life and destiny, based on an imposing set of facts and experimental proofs, to which new facts are added every day. Such a science, these tenets, all show more and more the reality of an invisible and incommensurable world, populated by living beings that had hitherto escaped our senses. And behold, new horizons are opening up, the prospects of our destiny are widening! We, ourselves, through the most important part of our beings, belong to this invisible world that is revealed to attentive observers every day. Cases of telepathy, of out-of-body experiences, of exteriorization of the living, and apparitions at a distance, so often narrated by F. W. H. Myers, C. Flammarion, Charles Richet, Dr. Dariex, Dr. J. Maxwell, and many others, have been abundantly demonstrated. The minutes of the British Society for Psychical Research are full to the brim with facts of this kind.

Spiritists believe that such an invisible and imponderable part of our individual personality, as an unalterable seat of our faculties and conscious self – in a word, what believers of all religions have called *soul* – survives death. It continues through time and space its evolution toward ever better states, which are ever more enlightened by rays of justice, truth, and eternal beauty. This soul, this conscious self, has as its indestructible shell, its vehicle, a fluidic body (i.e., the perispirit), a canvas of the human body, formed of subtle, radiant, invisible material, on which death has no action.

Here we find ourselves in presence of a theory, a conception capable of reconciling Materialistic and Spiritualistic tenets, which have for so long been at stake without being able to shake off or destroy each other. It states that the soul would no longer be a vague abstraction, but a center of strength and life, inseparable from its subtle, imponderable, though still material, form. This represents a positive basis for the high hopes and aspirations of humanity. Everything does not end with life for us: the self, forever perfectible, harvests in its constantly refined psychical state, the fruit of all its works, deeds, and self-sacrifices, built up in its previous lifetimes.

The doleful complaint, the cry of appeal rising to the sky from the depths of humanity, does not remain unanswered. Those who have lived among us, and now pursue in more etherealized forms their infinite evolution on the spiritual plane; these souls do not lose interest in our sufferings and tears. Summits of universal life constantly send toward

Earth currents of strength and inspiration. From thence come those flashes of genius and the powerful breaths that blow over the crowds at decisive moments. From there the comfort that soothes all those who are bent under the heavy burden of existence.

A mysterious link connects the visible to the invisible, the seen to the unseen. Our destiny is set on the grand chain of worlds. It results in gradual increases in life, intelligence, and sensitivity.

But the study of the concealed world is not without difficulties. There, as here, good and evil, truth and error, are all mingled, according to the degree of evolution of the spirits with which we come into contact. Hence the need to approach the field of experimentation with extreme caution, only after some preliminary theoretical studies. Spiritism is the science that regulates these rapports.

It teaches us how to discern, attract, and use the beneficial forces of the invisible world, to remove evil influences and, at the same time, to develop the hidden powers, the ignored faculties that lie dormant in the depths of every human being.

No. 6
ABOUT SPIRITIST EXPERIMENTS

→ Dr. Gustave Lebon took the initiative of offering a reward which seemed arbitrary: a prize of 500 French francs[84] was offered to the medium who, in full daylight, would produce a phenomenon of levitation before a qualified committee.

Why stipulate that it should be "in broad daylight," when it is of general knowledge that this type of phenomenon only takes place with attenuated light, since harsh light is known to exert a dissolving effect on psychical force?

---

84 [Trans. note] Over USD$2,000 in today's value. See French newspaper *La Matin*, May 29, 1908.

What would you say, readers of common sense, if an amateur suddenly demanded, in order to admit the existence of photography, that film should be developed in full light, when, until now, the chemical reactions involved require absolute shadow in the photographer's darkroom?

It should be pointed out that the complete darkness is by no means necessary for levitations; a dim red light should be sufficient to prevent any trickery or attempt of fraud. Besides, a number of other known natural phenomena also require a very dim light, if not darkness.

The impartial scientist will observe the law, the norm of a phenomenon, but be careful not to pretend to impose a priori conditions on its production.

Phenomena of levitation without contact of both furniture and people, and of casting molds of hands and faces, have been observed under such conditions that defy any criticism by scientists in France or elsewhere.

Photographs have been taken that are a very clear response to any suspicions of suggestion. After all, a photographic plate is not subject to hallucinations!

Many experiments are conducted in a strictly scientific manner; for example, those of Professor Filippo Bottazzi, director of the Institute of Physiology of the University of Naples (Italy), in May 1907, and witnessed by Professor Cardarelli (then a senator), among other scholars.

Of course, since our senses can be deceiving, recording equipment should be used to make it possible not only to establish the reality and objectivity of the phenomena, but also to provide graphs of physical force in action.

Now here are the measures obtained by the group of scientists mentioned above, in an experiment with famous medium Eusapia Paladino.

At the end of the room, behind a curtain, the following are placed in advance on a table:

1) A cylinder covered with paper blackened by smoke, free to turn around its vertical axis.
2) A letter-weighing balance.
3) A partly charged Zimmermann electric metronome.
4) A telegraph key connected to another electric signal.
5) A pear-shaped elastic rubber connected by means of a long, hard-walled rubber tube to a mercury manometer placed in the adjacent room.

As can be seen, these were truly fastidious precautions taken by the aforementioned learned scientists to make absolutely sure that they were not being deceived. So there! It was under such rigorous conditions that all those apparatuses designated above were impressed from a distance, while Eusapia's hands were held still by two of the experimenters, and all the sitters were forming a circle around her.

Twenty years ago, Eusapia was already operating as a medium in Milan (Italy) under the following circumstances:

The newspaper *Italia del Popolo*, of Milan, in its issue of November 18, 1892, featured a special supplement containing the minutes of seventeen seances held in that city. This document is signed by the following names: Schiaparelli, director of the Milan Astronomical Observatory; Aksakof (or Aksakov), Councilor of State to the Emperor of Russia; Professors Brofferio and Gerosa; Ermacora and G. Finzi, PhDs in Physics; Charles Richet, professor at the Faculty of Medicine of Paris and chief editor of *La Revue Scientifique*; and Lombroso, professor at the Faculty of Medicine of Turin.

These reports record the production of the following phenomena, obtained in darkened environment while the feet and the hands of the medium were continually held still by two of the sitters:

"Diverse objects, chairs, musical instruments, etc., moved without human contact; the imprint of fingers on clay; the apparition of hands against a luminous background; the apparition of phosphorescent lights; lifting of the medium on a table; chairs and their occupants being lifted; touches experienced by the spectators ..."

"In conclusion, the aforementioned witnesses declare that thanks to the precautions taken, no fraud was possible. They furthermore declare that, from what they had witnessed, there resulted 'the triumph of a truth which had been rendered unjustly unpopular.'"[85]

What splendor of language could equal the probative value of such a clear and concise style?

To these testimonies, one could add hundreds of others of equal value. Will they be void in the eyes of our adversaries, and will it be necessary to refer to these experiments every time a new skeptical demand is made?

Eusapia's sittings have presented many other even more important phenomena.

"More recently, professor Lombroso, while giving an account of his experiments in the Italian magazine *Arena* [February 1908], reported the following facts:"

"'After the transport of a very heavy object, Eusapia, in a state of trance, said to me: "Why do you waste your time with these trifles? I am able to show you your mother; but it is necessary that you concentrate intensely on her." Dominated by this promise, after half an hour of meeting had transpired, I was drawn by an intense desire to see it achieved. The table seemed to give its approval, with its usual movements of successive risings, to my intimate thought. Suddenly, under a half reddish light, I saw a short leaning form leaving from within the curtains, as had been that of my mother, covered by a glazed veil. She came around the table until she approached and stopped next

---

[85] [Trans. note] Excerpted from L. DENIS, *After Death* (Trans. G. G. Fleurot, J. Korngold. New York: USSF, 2017), p. 173.

to me, murmuring words that several people heard, but that my own particular hearing deficiency did not enable me to receive. Then, as if under the influence of a sharp emotion, I begged her to repeat their words. She then said to me: 'Cæsar, fio mio!' what, I acknowledge that it was not her ordinary way of saying it. Indeed, being Venetian, she would have said: *mio fiol*; then, drawing aside her veil, she gave me a kiss.'"

"Lombroso then points out the communications, written or spoken, in foreign languages, the revelations of unknown facts as well of the medium and of the assistants, and the facts about telepathy."[86]

Finally, to conclude this note, let us move to Great Britain, where the ghost of Katie King was photographed by Sir W. Crookes, destroying any suspicion of *suggestion*.

"Under the name of cross-correspondence, British experimenters devised a new method of communication through mediumistic writing, which would be able to establish, in a more precise way, the identity of the communicating spirits. Sir Oliver Lodge, Rector of the University of Birmingham, reported on these experiences in his address to the Society for Psychical Research on January 30, 1908:

"'We find the late Edmund Gurney and the late Richard Hodgson and the late F. W. H. Myers, with some other less known names, constantly purporting to communicate with us, with the express purpose of patiently proving their identity. We also find them answering specific questions in a manner characteristic of their known personalities, and giving evidence of knowledge appropriate to them ...'"

"'The ostensible communicators realize the need of such proof just as fully as we do, and have do their best to satisfy the rational demand. Some of us think they have

---

86 [Trans. note] Excerpted from L. DENIS, *After Death* (Trans. G. G. Fleurot, J. Korngold. New York: USSF, 2017), p. 175.

already succeeded; others are still doubtful.' "I am one of those who, though they would like to see further and still stronger and more continued proofs, are of the opinion that a good case has been made out, and that, as the best working hypothesis at the present time, it is legitimate to grant that lucid moments of [interchange] with deceased persons may in the best cases supervene amid a mass of supplementary material ...'"

"'Cross-correspondence,' continues Sir Oliver, '– that is, the reception of part of a message through one medium and part through another, neither portion separately being understood by either – is good evidence of one intelligence dominating both automatists. And if the message is characteristic of some one particular deceased person, and is received as such by people to whom he was not intimately known, then it is fair proof of the continued intellectual activity of that person. If, further, we get from him a piece of literary criticism which is eminently in his vein, and has not occurred to ordinary people, then I say the proof, already striking, is tending to become crucial. These are the kinds of proof which the Society has had communicated to it. The boundary between the two states – the present and the future – is still substantial, but it is wearing thin in places. Like excavators engaged in boring a tunnel from opposite ends, amid the roar of water and other noises we are beginning to hear, now and again, the strokes of the pickaxes of our comrades on the other side.'"[87]

To all these testimonies, I may add my own. Thirty years of rigorous experimentation, pursued in various milieus, with many subjects (mediums), have shown me that, if the so-called psychical phenomena can be partly explained by the externalization of forces emanating from the living,

---

[87] [Trans. note] Excerpted from L. Denis, *Into the Unseen* (Trans. H. M. Monteiro. New York: USSF, 2017), pp. 286–288.

a significant number of these facts find an explanation only in the intervention of invisible entities. These are none other than the spirits of the dead; they subsist in a subtle, imponderable form, whose elements belong to etherealized matter.

Therefore, the Spiritist explanation is the only one that gives a complete answer to the reality of phenomena considered in their many aspects. It provides us with proof that an ocean of invisible life surrounds and envelops us; and that, in the hereafter, all human beings finds themselves in the fullness of their faculties and consciousness.

No. 7
ABOUT THE ROLE PLAYED BY MEDIUMS
DURING MANIFESTATIONS

→ In the monthly journal *Écho du Merveilleux* of October 1910, writer Jules Bois makes the following proposition: "This constant need for a medium, and this law according which the metapsychical fact results from the medium, is accomplished in the medium and by the medium."

Mr. Bois does not exclude the possibility of an intervention of deeper causes, but whether it is autosuggestion, other forms of suggestion, or interventions of extraneous forces, in his view, the vehicle is always the living human being.

This proposition, albeit exact in many cases, should not be generalized. Professor Lombroso, after a careful investigation of phenomena of obsession, said (see *The Annals of Psychical Science*, vol. VII, no.40, p. 177, April 1908):

"In 'haunted houses,' where suddenly bottles, tables, chairs, etc., are seen to move, no one talks about the influence of a medium, since it is often in uninhabited houses that these phenomena occur for many generations, and even for centuries."

Like J. Bois and G. Lebon, Lombroso had long sought the cause of Spiritist phenomena in the mediums themselves, and attributed these manifestations to the action of forces emanating from the subjects (i.e., the mediums).

However, a large number of facts observed by Lombroso during new experiments came to invalidate this hypothesis and to demonstrate its insufficiency.

At first, it was the simultaneity of certain phenomena during seances: it was not plausible to admit that the psychical force of a medium was able to transform itself simultaneously and at the same time into a driving force and a sensory force, and still act at the same time in several different directions and for different purposes.

First of all, there was the simultaneity of certain phenomena during seances to be considered: one could not possibly conceive of a medium's psychical force being able to transform itself simultaneously and at the same instant into both a driving force and a sensory force, while at the same time still acting in several different directions and for completely different purposes.

Then there are facts that occur against the will of the medium, against the will of the sitters, and even against the will of the spirit entity that is communicating. A will can therefore intervene in Spiritist phenomena, whose origin cannot be found in any of the human organisms gathered in the seance room.

In trance phenomena, intelligent motives and energies are manifest, which are extraneous, superior and disproportionate to those of the medium.

As for cases of full levitation of, for example, a medium, they cannot be explained by the action of a force coming from the subject who rises above the ground. Actually, the gravity center of a body would not be able to move through space, were it not for an external force acting upon this body.

Here is what Dr. Venzano says about simultaneous occurrence of phenomena (see *The Annals of Psychical Science*, vol. VII, no. 40, p. 174, April 1908):

"During a seance at Milan, when Eusapia was at her deepest condition of trance, we saw appear on the right, I myself and those next to me, the image of a beloved woman, who said to me one confused word, 'treasure' it seemed like to me. In the middle was Eusapia asleep near us, up above the curtain swelled out several times; at the same time on the left a table moved in the cabinet, and from it a small object was transported on to the table in the middle...."

"Dr. Imoda observed that whilst a phantom took out of M. Becker's hand a pen and returned it to him another phantom rested its brow on that of Imoda."

"On another occasion, whilst I was caressed by a phantom, Princess Ruspoli felt herself touched on the head by a hand ..."

It is inconceivable that the psychical force of a medium would be able to act at the same time in three different directions. How could one concentrate an action strong enough to obtain plastic phenomena on three separate points?

The same observation applies to direct writing phenomena. One day, in Orange (France), at midday, in the heart of summer, while all life seemed suspended outside, and one could only hear the song of the cicadas and the complaints of the wind, I was sitting near a table at a friend's house – a novelty merchant – with two other people busy writing and bending over their paperwork. Suddenly, I saw a sliver of paper, which seemed to be coming out of the ceiling, descending into the void space over my head, until it slowly fell into my hat, lying on the table next to me.

Two lines of fine writing, two verses, were inscribed therein. They contained a warning, a prediction about me that has come true since. I am convinced that the two people present had no part in this phenomenon, that we cannot explain it by suggestion or subconsciousness.

Faithful to the experimental method, I will now present some facts establishing the reality of extraneous interventions and providing indications of their nature and identity. These facts, in fact seem much more eloquent to me than all the commentaries.

So, without further ado, here is a quote of the original written minutes that I have in my hands:

"'On the January 13, 1899, twelve persons had met at Mr. David's, located at the Place des Corps-Saints, in Avignon (France), for their weekly Spiritualist seance.'"

"'After a moment of reflection, the entranced medium Mrs. Gallas was seen turning to talk to the ecclesiastic Father Grimaud, speaking to him in the sign language used by certain speech-impaired, profoundly deaf individuals. The spirit's gesturing skills were such that it was asked to communicate more slowly, which it promptly did. By a precautionary measure which proved to be commendably unobtrusive, Mr. Grimaud merely uttered the letters as they were transmitted by the medium. Since each isolated letter meant nothing, it was impossible, even if one had so wished, to interpret the spirit's message, which was disclosed only at the end of the communication, when it was read by one of the two group members who were in charge of transcribing the alphabetic characters.'"

"'Moreover, the medium employed a double method, which consists in enunciating all the letters of a word, to indicate its spelling, a form only sensible to the observer's eyes, and another technique which expresses articulated words without taking into account their written form, a method once devised by Friar Fourcade, and which was in use exclusively at the Institution for the Speech-impaired and Profoundly Deaf of Avignon. These details are provided by Father Grimaud, director and founder of that establishment.'"

"'The communication concerning the highly philanthropic work to which Father Grimaud has been devoted was signed: Friar Fourcade, deceased in Caen. *None of the participants, with the exception of the venerable Father, ever knew or could possibly have known the author of this communication – although he had spent some time in Avignon some thirty years earlier – or his method.'*"

"It was signed by the group members present at the sitting; Mr. Toursier, retired director of the Banque de France; Mr. Roussel, music leader with the 58th Infantry; Mr. Domenach, lieutenant of the 58th Infantry; Mr. David, a businessman; Misters Brémond and Canuel; Mmes. Toursier, Roussel, David, and Brémond."

"The following certificate was then attached to the written minutes:"

"'I, the undersigned, Grimaud, priest, founding director of the Institution for the Speech-impaired and Profoundly Deaf and Children with Learning Disabilities of Avignon, hereby certify that all of the above is true and absolutely correct. I really must state that I was far from expecting such a communication, whose importance I fully recognize from the point of view of the reality of Spiritism, of which I am a fervent adept, and have no difficulty in thus publicly declaring.

Avignon, April 17, 1899.
Signed: Grimaud, priest.'"[88]

Moreover, worth mentioning is a photographed apparition of a Boer, as recounted by W. Stead, the great English publisher. This Boer, named Piet Botha, was completely unknown to him, and only later was recognized by several

---

[88] [Trans. note] Léon DENIS, *Into the Unseen* (Trans. H. M. Monteiro. New York: USSF, 2017), pp. 318–320.

delegates from South Africa, who had come to England (see *La Revue Scientifique et Morale du Spiritisme*, vol. XV, p. 529, January 1909).

The following facts should also be added: the case of Blanche Abercrombie, cited by F. W. H. Myers in *Human Personality* and which cannot be explained either by suggestion or by subconsciousness; the same is true of the case reported by Dr. Isaac K. Funk (*The Annals of Psychical Science*, vol. VII, no. 40, p. 204, April 1908); the case of Evangelides, a message obtained from a deceased person (whose death was not known to anyone) by Miss Laura – daughter of Judge John W. Edmonds of New York – in modern Greek language, unknown to the medium (*The Annals of Psychical Science*, vol. VII, no. 40, p. 178, April 1908); and the case of direct writing by Dr. Roman Uricz, chief physician of the hospital of Bialy-Kamien, in former Galicia, as reported in detail in my book *Christianity and Spiritism* (see also *La Revue Spirite*, April 1907).